Windows 7:
Troubleshooting Made Easy

Agora Business Publications LLP

Published by Agora Business Publications LLP

Agora Business Publications LLP
Nesfield House
Broughton Hall Business Park
Skipton
BD23 3AN

Publisher: Victoria Burrill
Author: Stefan Johnson

Phone: 01756 693 180
Fax: 01756 693 196
Email: cs@agorapublications.co.uk
Web: www.agorabusinesspublications.co.uk

ISBN: 978-1-908245-02-1

Copyright © 2011 Agora Business Publications LLP.

The contents of *Windows 7: Troubleshooting Made Easy* are copyright protected. No part of this publication may be reproduced or transmitted in any form, or stored in any retrieval system without permission from the publisher. All rights reserved.

Microsoft, Office and Windows are Registered Trademarks of Microsoft Corporation. All other trademarks are acknowledged as belonging to their respective companies.

This book has been created with the utmost care. However, the publishers are not responsible and do not give any guarantees or legal responsibilities for the successful use of the information contained within. The publishers do not accept responsibility for the error-free operation within the user's system environment. There is absolutely no claim to be made for consequent damages or deficiency.

Agora Business Publications LLP. Nesfield House, Broughton Hall Business Park, Skipton, Yorkshire, BD23 3AN. Registered in England No. OC323533, VAT No. GB 893 3184 95.

Table of Contents

Introduction v

1: New Rescue Functions in Windows 7
    4 Quick Essential Fixes to Help You on the Road to Recovery 1
    Fix 1: Use System Restore from Safe Mode to Undo
    Damaging Changes to Your PC 3
    Fix 2: Revert to the Last Working Configuration 4
    Fix 3: Restore Your System via the Windows DVD 5
    Fix 4: Repair a Failed Hard Drive Boot Sector 8
    Track Down the Cause of Serious Errors in the Event Logs 11
    Essential Steps to Make Your System Stable Again 12

2: Diagnose and Cure System Problems in Windows 7
    Quickly Fix Common Windows 7 Set-up Problems 17
    Restore Missing Windows Applications 18
    Repair a Missing CD/DVD Drive in Windows 7 19
    Fix Problems When Your iPod/iPhone Won't Sync with iTunes 20
    Revert to the Old Style Windows Interface to Use Programs
    Incompatible with Aero 21
    Correct Problem-solving with the Windows Command
    Line Interface 22
    Crucial Steps to Troubleshoot Serious System Errors 23

3: Essential Steps to Remove Hard Drive Errors
    Prevent Data Loss: Diagnose and Fix Problems 27
    Free Wasted Hard Drive Space by Deleting Duplicates
    and Leftover Files 29
    Safely Manage Your Hard Drive Partitions to Avoid Data Loss 32
    Fast Fixes for Hard Drive Maintenance Problems 33

4: Dispose of and Cure Serious Network and Internet Problems
    2 Quick Checks to See if a Website is Working 35
    Discover the 7 Problems that Can Stop You Surfing 36
    Fast Fixes for Network Adapter Issues 37
    Resolve Network Protocol Corruptions with Ease 39
    Cure IP Address Renewal Failure Using DHCP 40
    Trouble Going Online via Wi-Fi? Use this Fix 42
    Windows 7 Tips to Fix Problems with Old Routers 44

5: 7 Essential Tools for Windows Error Elimination
Discover the Hidden Meaning of Cryptic Error Messages 47
Cure Windows Problems Using SiSoft Sandra 49
Solve Startup Problems to Fix a Non-booting PC 50
Repair Serious Registry Corruptions Before they Crash Your PC 52
Fix Problems via the Action Center in Windows 7 54
Quickly Repair Corrupt User Profile Associations 55
Repair Audio Problems Experienced While Playing DVD Movies 56

6: Safely Dispose of Windows 7 STOP Errors
Dealing with the Dreaded Blue Screen of Death 59
Quick Cures for STOP Errors in Windows 7 60
Essential Steps to Cure Serious STOP Errors 61
Easily Cure Device-related Blue Screens 65
Crucial Steps to Cure Problems with the Windows 7 Kernel 67
Fast Fixes for Driver-related STOP Errors 69
Prevent Constant Windows 7 Re-boots Caused by
Blue Screen Crashes 71

7: Quickly Repair Problems with DLL Files in Windows 7
Getting to the Bottom of DLL Errors 73
3 Quick Fixes to Resolve DLL Errors 74
Stop Orphaned DLLs Cluttering Your System with DLLArchive 75
Cure Problems with Locked DLL Files 77
Re-register Missing DLLs with RegSvr32 78

Windows 7:
Troubleshooting Made Easy

Dear Windows User,

When you have Windows 7 problems, there is only one thing that can really help: specially selected step-by-step instructions and professional troubleshooting tools which you can use to quickly restore your system. It's essential to get your PC back up and running as fast as possible, since if your system refuses to work, you won't have any access to your emails or the Internet. Of course, it's even more stressful if you also need your PC for work.

In this book, you will find the professional tools and repair techniques which will allow you to successfully and quickly restore your Windows 7 system in case of emergency. If a serious system crash occurs, you will immediately be able to rescue your computer and even prevent serious system crashes from taking place in the future – and that's just in the first chapter, New Rescue Functions in Windows 7.

There's much more to discover in the other chapters that follow:

- Diagnose and Cure System Problems in Windows 7
- Essential Steps to Remove Hard Drive Errors
- Dispose of and Cure Serious Network and Internet Problems
- 7 Essential Tools for Windows Error Elimination
- Safely Dispose of STOP Errors
- Quickly Repair Problems with DLL Files

Best regards,

Stefan Johnson

1: New Rescue Functions in Windows 7

If you can't boot Windows 7 then you still have a few options available to cure the problem, thanks to Windows built-in disaster recovery tools. If you've installed software or hardware that was incompatible with your PC, you may find that it's impossible to get Windows to load properly, in order to remove the incompatible application or driver.

Fortunately, Microsoft provides recovery tools to help you repair a failed Windows system, but they can be tricky to use. In this chapter, we will cover a complete guide to restoring a failed Windows system using little-known tools and techniques. Just follow the simple flowchart (see page 2) to help you identify your PC problem and quickly apply the appropriate fix.

4 Quick Essential Fixes to Help You on the Road to Recovery

A corrupt Windows 7 system will usually only allow you to get part way through the boot process, thereby preventing access to the Windows desktop. Apart from problems with essential devices, such as the hard drive or RAM (which are discussed later), the errors that prevent Windows from booting are usually caused by one of the three events described below:

1. **Recent software installation** – if you install a new software application on to your system and then find that Windows will no longer boot up properly, it is likely that the new application has added a setting to your registry that is causing the boot process to fail. To cure the problem, you need to revert your system to an earlier working version of the registry.

2. **Recent hardware installation** – if your problem with Windows occurs after you have installed a new hardware device, then it is likely that the problem is either caused by the device itself, or by an incompatible device driver. The former problem is usually easy to resolve – simply disconnect the new hardware device. If that doesn't work, then you will need to remove the problem device and reset your system to an earlier working configuration.

3. **Corrupt boot record** – the boot sector of your hard drive contains a small piece of code needed by your PC to load Windows. If this, or any of the associated files, become corrupt, you will need to replace them with fresh copies.

How you cure these different errors depends on how far you can get through the Windows 7 boot process. Use the following flowchart to decide on the right recovery option, based on how far your PC can progress through the boot sequence, and then turn to the appropriate fix in this chapter.

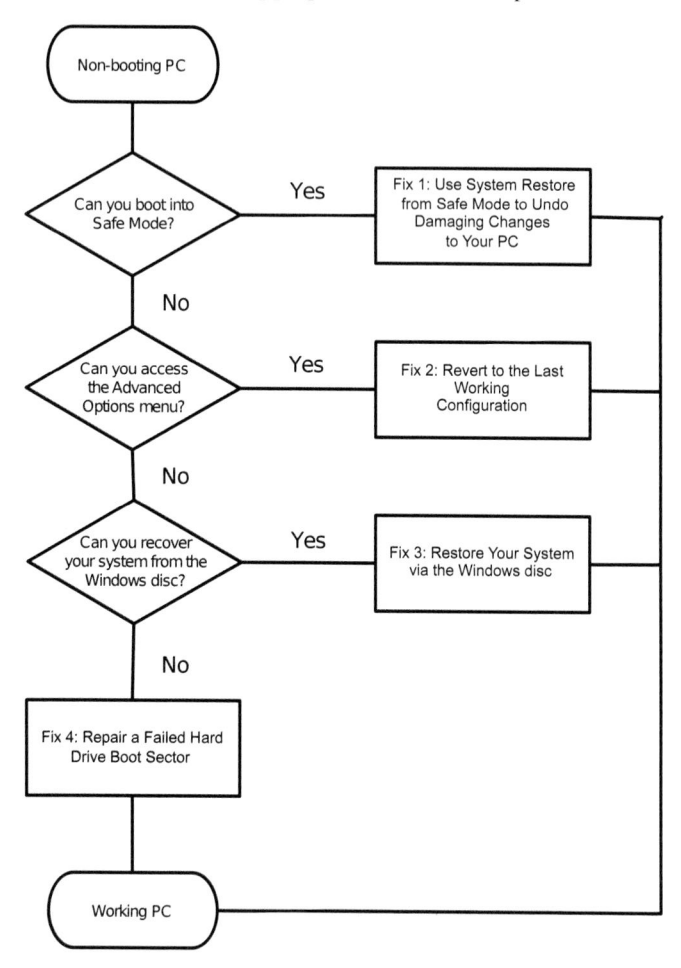

```
                    Non-booting PC
                          |
                          v
            Can you boot into      Yes      Fix 1: Use System Restore
              Safe Mode?          ----->    from Safe Mode to Undo
                                            Damaging Changes
                                            to Your PC
                          | No
                          v
            Can you access         Yes      Fix 2: Revert to the Last
             the Advanced         ----->    Working
             Options menu?                  Configuration
                          | No
                          v
            Can you recover        Yes      Fix 3: Restore Your System
           your system from the   ----->    via the Windows disc
             Windows disc?
                          | No
                          v
            Fix 4: Repair a Failed Hard
                Drive Boot Sector
                          |
                          v
                    Working PC
```

Quickly resolve your system problems by following the flowchart

When working through the flowchart, try the solution appropriate to the boot problem your PC is experiencing. If that solution doesn't immediately repair Windows, it should still allow you to get further through the boot process. You should therefore work through the flowchart again, from the boot step you can now access.

> If you've tried all of the steps in the flowchart above and still can't get your PC to work, it is likely that one of the fundamental pieces of your PC's hardware is faulty, such as the hard drive or the RAM. If this is the case, then you will need to replace the problematic hardware device causing the problem. Try removing all non-essential hardware components from your system and attach them one at a time to find out which is the problem.

Fix 1: Use System Restore from Safe Mode to Undo Damaging Changes to Your PC

If your PC can boot to Windows Safe Mode, but you are still experiencing errors, then the simplest way to fix the problem is by using Windows System Restore to revert your system to its previous configuration, before you made any changes.

To do this, first you need to start your system in Safe Mode, by following the steps below:

1. Switch your PC on and hold down the [**F8**] key, then press [**F8**] again.

2. When the Advanced Options menu appears, select **Safe Mode** using the [**Up Arrow**] and [**Down Arrow**] keys and then press [**Enter**] to select the option.

3. If you have multiple versions of Windows installed on the same PC, you will now be asked to choose which one you are having problems with. Choose the version of Windows that is causing problems and press [**Enter**].

4. If prompted to log in, select your Administrator account, and enter the Administrator's password, if one is set.

Once you are in Safe Mode, you can repair your Windows 7 system as follows:

1. In Safe Mode, click **Start > All Programs > Accessories > System Tools > System Restore**.

2. Click **Next**.

3. Select a restore point from before you made the change that is causing you problems ① and click **Next** ②.

4. Click **Finish**. Your PC will be restored and will revert to the older configuration.

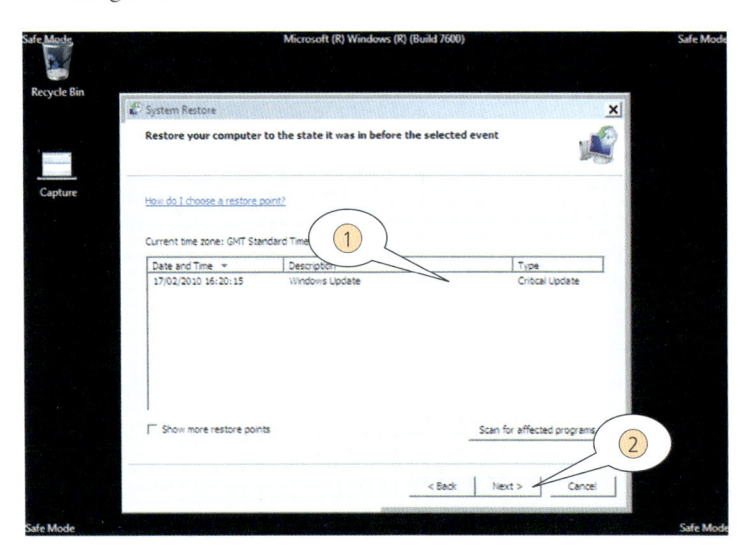

Use System Restore to revert to a previous configuration

> If your problem still isn't cured, you can reload System Restore by repeating the steps given above, and then try reverting to an even earlier restore point.

Fix 2: Revert to the Last Working Configuration

If Windows 7 won't start at all, meaning that you can't access Safe Mode to run the System Restore tool, you still have several options to repair your machine. If you can access the Advanced Options menu by pressing [**F8**] when your

PC is turned on, you will hopefully be able to revert Windows to the working configuration that the system used to boot – in effect, reverting your system to the last successful set of settings.

To do this, use the following steps:

1. Switch your PC on and hold down the [**F8**] key, then press [**F8**] again.

2. When the Advanced Options menu appears, select **Last Known Good Configuration** using the [**Up Arrow**] and [**Down Arrow**] keys ③ and then press [**Enter**] to select the option.

3. Your PC will start Windows with the last set of settings known to work. Once Windows starts, you can undo whatever changes were made that caused the system to become unstable in the first place.

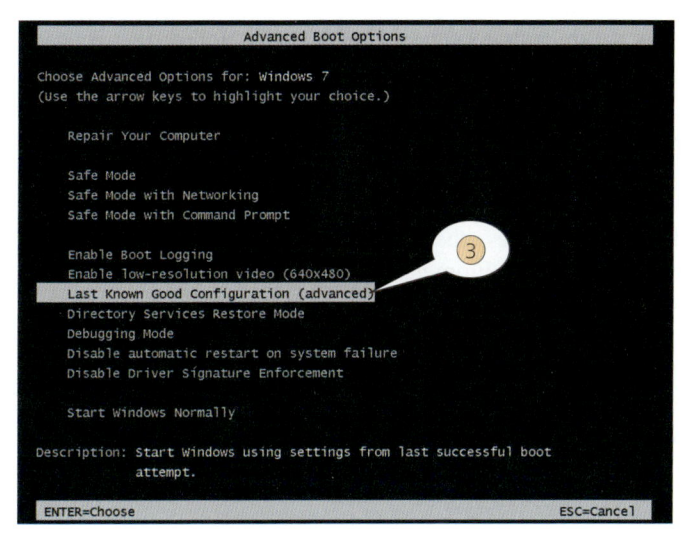

```
                    Advanced Boot Options
Choose Advanced Options for: windows 7
(Use the arrow keys to highlight your choice.)

    Repair Your Computer

    Safe Mode
    Safe Mode with Networking
    Safe Mode with Command Prompt

    Enable Boot Logging
    Enable low-resolution video (640x480)
    Last Known Good Configuration (advanced)    ③
    Directory Services Restore Mode
    Debugging Mode
    Disable automatic restart on system failure
    Disable Driver Signature Enforcement

    Start Windows Normally

Description: Start Windows using settings from last successful boot
             attempt.

ENTER=Choose                                         ESC=Cancel
```

Repair your system via the Advanced Options menu

Fix 3: Restore Your System via the Windows DVD

If your PC refuses to boot even to the Advanced Options menu, or restoring your PC to its last working configuration doesn't work, then all is not lost. Microsoft usefully provides recovery tools for Windows on the Windows 7 installation DVD, so you should be able to recover a non-booting system by starting your PC from your Windows installation disc.

Before doing this, you need to make sure that your computer is configured to boot from CD/DVD. This is done in the BIOS as follows:

1. Re-boot your PC and press the [**F2**] or [**DEL**] key as instructed when you see the BIOS menu option appear on-screen.

2. Use the [**Up Arrow**] and [**Down Arrow**] keys to select the **Advanced BIOS Features** option and press [**Enter**].

3. Set your CD/DVD drive to be the first boot device using the arrow keys.

4. Press [**F10**] to save your changes and exit.

With the computer set to boot from the CD/DVD drive, follow the recovery options appropriate to your system below.

Run System Restore from the Windows 7 Installation DVD

Windows 7 allows you to access the System Recovery Options menu from the Windows installation DVD. From here, you can run the regular Windows System Restore tool to revert your system to a previous restore point, created before the software or hardware that is causing your system to refuse to boot was installed.

To access the tool, follow these steps:

1. Place your Windows 7 installation DVD in your CD/DVD drive and restart your computer.

2. When your computer boots from the DVD you will see the message **Press any key to boot from CD or DVD**. Press [**Enter**].

3. Set the Time and Currency format options to **English (United Kingdom)**. Click **Next**.

4. When prompted with the Windows 7 install screen, click **Repair your computer**.

5. Select the option **Use recovery tools that can help fix problems starting Windows**, select your Windows installation in the list and click **Next**.

6. Click **System Restore** ④.

7. Click **Next**.

8. Select a restore point from before you made the change that is causing you problems and click **Next**.

9. Click **Finish**. Your PC will be restored and will revert to the older configuration.

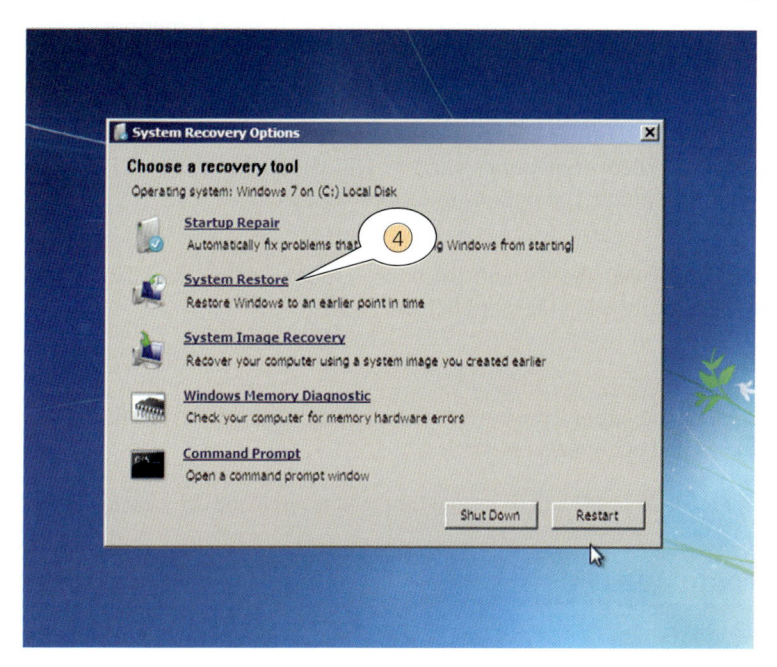

Use the System Recovery menu to fix Windows 7

Restore Your System Without a Windows 7 DVD

If you didn't have a Windows 7 installation DVD supplied with your PC, it is possible that instead your PC manufacturer pre-installed the System Recovery Options menu on your system. If so, you can access it via the Advanced Options menu as follows:

New Rescue Functions in Windows 7   7

1. Remove all floppy disks, CDs, and DVDs from your computer and then restart.

2. As your computer boots up hold down the [**F8**] key, then press [**F8**] again.

3. When the Advanced Options menu appears, select **Repair your computer** using the [**Up Arrow**] and [**Down Arrow**] keys, and then press [**Enter**]. If 'Repair your computer' is not listed as an option, then your computer does not include the System Recovery Options menu as a pre-installed recovery option.

4. Set the keyboard layout for your PC – **English (United Kingdom)** – then click **Next**.

5. Click on your username and enter your password, then click **OK**.

6. The System Recovery Options window will be displayed. From here, you can choose a number of options to restore your PC.

Once you've opened the System Recovery Options menu, run the System Restore tool by following the steps below:

1. Click **Next**.

2. Select a restore point from before you made the change that is causing you problems and click **Next**.

3. Click **Finish**. Your PC will be restored and will revert to the older configuration.

> If you see a warning message telling you that your PC has been reverted to an earlier time, simply click **OK**.

Fix 4: Repair a Failed Hard Drive Boot Sector

The Boot Sector of your hard drive contains the code that your PC needs to execute in order to load Windows 7. This piece of code tells your PC, via the BIOS, where to find the core component of Windows 7, the Kernel, in order to load it into memory.

Once the Kernel has been loaded, it then proceeds to load up all of the background services and eventually, the Windows desktop.

If the Boot Sector of your hard drive becomes damaged or goes missing, then Windows will fail to load even into Safe Mode, and you will be presented with an error message similar to the following:

```
File: \Boot\Bcd
Status: 0xc000000f
Info: An error occurred while attempting to read
the boot configuration data.
```

Or you might see the following:

```
NTLDR is missing
Press any key to restart
```

If you see this error, or you can't even get your PC to boot into Safe Mode using the steps given earlier, then you will need to repair the Boot Sector. Fortunately, the System Restore Options menu in Windows 7 gives you the ability to do this.

Repair the Boot Sector in Windows 7

If you are experiencing boot time error messages that won't let you start Windows 7, the first thing to try is the Startup Repair tool, which you can access as follows:

1. Open the System Restore Options menu using the steps given previously.

2. Click on **Startup Repair**. The Startup Repair wizard will launch.

3. The wizard will automatically scan your PC for startup problems, and depending on what problems are found, you could be prompted to answer a series of questions to help fix the problem.

4. Click through the steps of the wizard, then click **Restart** when the problem has been fixed.

> Startup Repair should automatically apply all the hard drive fixes that you need.

If the Startup Repair tool cannot help resolve your startup problem, you can still repair the Boot Sector of the hard drive manually from the command prompt. To do so, first re-install the Windows boot loader by following these steps:

1. Open the System Restore Options menu in the Recovery Environment using the steps given previously.

2. Click on **Command Prompt**. The command line window will open.

3. At the prompt type **BCDEDIT /exp ort C:\BCD_Backup** and press [**Enter**]. This will backup your BCD to the file C:\BCD_Backup.

4. At the prompt type **C:** then press [**Enter**]. Type **CD boot** then press [**Enter**]. The prompt will change to C:\boot>.

5. Type **ATTRIB bcd -s -h –r** and press [**Enter**], then rename the original BCD file with the command **REN c:\boot\bcd bcd.old** followed by [**Enter**].

6. Now, rebuild the BCD with the command **BOOTREC /RebuildBcd**. This will search your hard drive for installations of Windows, and build a boot menu allowing you to switch between them.

7. Type **EXIT** and press [**Enter**] to re-boot your system.

Once you have re-installed the Windows 7 boot loader, you should also repair your hard drive's Master Boot Record as follows:

1. Open the System Restore Options menu in the Recovery Environment using the steps given previously.

2. Click on **Command Prompt**. The command prompt window will open.

3. At the command prompt type **BOOTREC /FixMbr** and press [**Enter**].

4. Next, at the command prompt type **BOOTREC /FixBoot** and press [**Enter**].

5. Type **EXIT** and press [**Enter**] to re-boot your system.

When your PC re-boots, the Boot Sector of the hard drive will be repaired and

Windows will load normally. Make sure that you've removed the Windows installation DVD if it's still in the drive.

Track Down the Cause of Serious Errors in the Event Logs

Once you've dealt with the pressing problem of a non-booting Windows 7 system, you really need to track down the cause of the problem to ensure that it doesn't reoccur. Windows stores details of the majority of the problems that it encounters in the Event Log (if the problem was related to the hard drive Boot Sector, it won't be recorded, since the hard drive cannot be accessed).

The Event Log will record the name of the program, Windows component or hardware driver that caused the problem. If you've restored your system using a restore point, then the problematic software or driver should have been removed, but you should still check on what was causing the problem in case you try to install it again.

You can access the Event Log Viewer by following the steps below:

1. Click **Start > Control Panel**.

2. Double-click on **Administrative Tools**, then **Event Viewer**.

3. Expand the Windows Logs subtree in the left-hand column (5), then double-click on the **System** error group.

4. Click on the **Date and Time** column heading (6) to sort the events in order of their occurrence.

5. Search through the list of events to find any that occurred at the time your PC failed to start up.

6. Select any such events that you find, then click **Details > Friendly View**. It's likely that the description of the event will provide troubleshooting clues to the cause of your PC's instability.

7. Repeat steps 3–6 for the Applications error group.

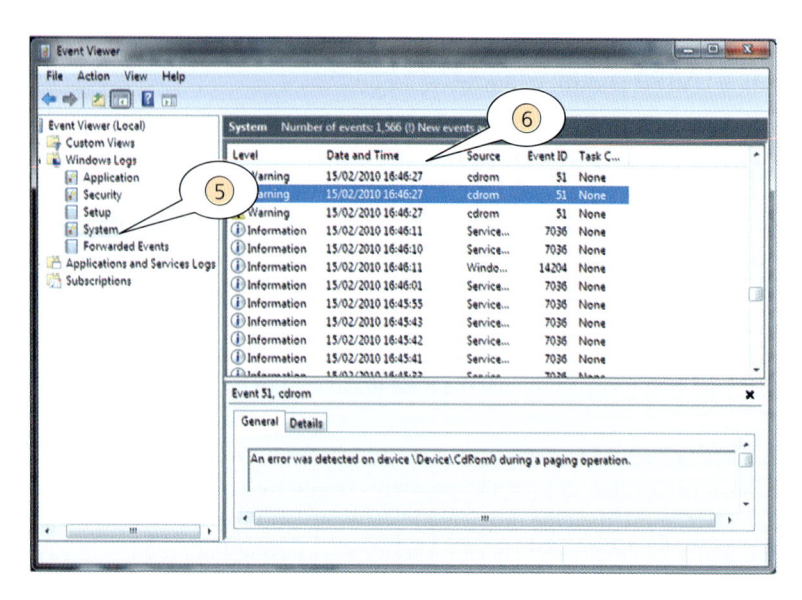

Check for problems in the Event Viewer

> You can use the **Action** > **Find** menu option to search for a particular error event.

Essential Steps to Make Your System Stable Again

Once you've recovered a failed PC, there are certain steps you should take to ensure that your PC stays stable. You should start off by checking the integrity of your hard drive and repair any errors, then check your essential system files are intact, and finally check your system's RAM and repair your registry.

Detect and Repair Hard Drive Errors

To find and fix Windows hard drive errors, you can use the built-in hard drive checking utility as follows:

1. Open **Computer**, right-click on your **C:** drive and choose **Properties**.

2. Click on the **Tools** tab, then click **Check Now**.

12   New Rescue Functions in Windows 7

3. Tick **Automatically fix file system errors** and **Scan for and attempt recovery of bad sectors**, then click **Start**.

4. Click **Yes** to schedule the drive check for the next time you restart your PC.

5. Restart your PC and the drive check will run before Windows loads.

Check the Integrity of Your Windows System Files

Corrupt or missing system files can be the cause of Windows problems and crashes, but the System File Checker can cure such problems by replacing problem system files with pristine new copies from your Windows 7 installation DVD.

To complete this fix, you will need to have your Windows installation DVD to hand, then proceed as follows:

1. Click **Start > All Programs > Accessories**, right-click on **Command Prompt** and choose **Run as administrator**.

2. At the command prompt type **SFC /SCANNOW** and press [**Enter**].

3. The System File Checker will start. If prompted to, insert your Windows installation DVD into the drive.

4. When the file check has completed, re-boot your system.

> If you don't have a Windows 7 installation DVD, your PC manufacturer may have pre-installed copies of the files needed by System File Checker on to your hard drive. You should still try running the steps above, even if you don't have a Windows 7 DVD – if the files have been pre-installed, System File Checker won't ask for the DVD.

Repair Your PC's Registry

As settings are added and removed, your PC's registry can become corrupted, with orphaned settings left by software that has long since been removed. This can cause system crashes and a slow down in performance, so after recovering your broken system, repair your registry using Little Registry Cleaner, which you download here: http://tiny.cc/d6tgw.

To use the tool:

1. Open Little Registry Cleaner and click **Yes** if prompted to create a restore point.

2. Click **Scan registry** (7). A list of all of the problems with your registry will be displayed.

3. Click **Fix problems** > **Yes** (8) to repair the registry problems.

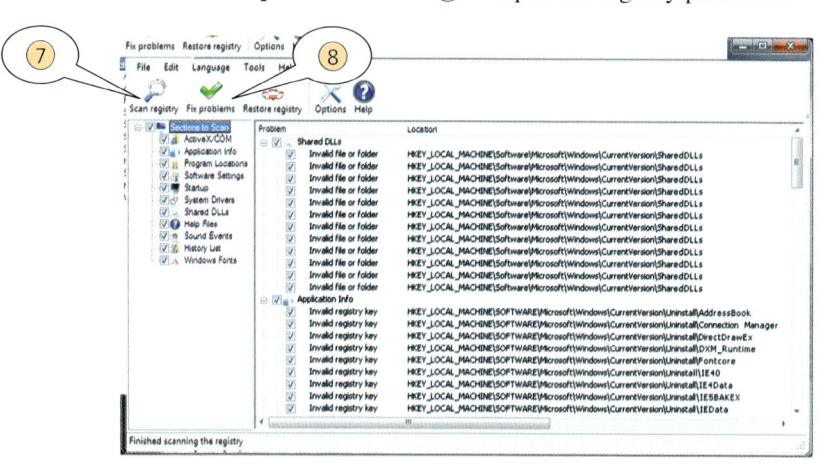

Repair your registry with Little Registry Cleaner

Check Your System RAM for Errors

Faulty system RAM can be one of the hardest problems to detect, as it is often manifested in random system crashes with no obvious cause. If your PC still seems unstable after you have followed the recovery steps in this chapter, you should run a memory checker to scan your PC's RAM for problems.

Windows 7 has a built-in tool that can be simply used to check for memory errors – the Windows Memory Diagnostics tool, built into the System Recovery Options menu. Simply load the System Recovery Options menu by following the steps given on page 8, then click on **Windows Memory Diagnostics** and follow the prompts.

> If you find any problems with your system's RAM, you will need to replace the faulty memory module to cure the problem.

There's nothing more frustrating than finding your PC won't boot, since, without Windows, how can you track down the problem? Fortunately, there are ways, which we've shown you in this chapter. Using our unique troubleshooting flowchart and tips, you can cure any non-booting Windows 7 system in a matter of minutes, regardless of which Windows 7 version you have.

2: Diagnose and Cure System Problems in Windows 7

Even with its much improved performance and state-of-the-art feature set, Windows 7 is far from perfect. If you've purchased a new computer that has Windows 7 pre-installed on it, or perhaps upgraded your existing PC from an older version of Windows, you may have already run into problems.

Whether you've encountered simple niggles that have presented more of an annoyance than anything, or other issues that have been more serious, this chapter covers a wide array of common Windows 7 problems. By reading this chapter, you will be able to quickly solve common obstacles, ranging from installation and set-up issues, all the way through to enhancing your set-up by adding missing features and tweaking hidden settings.

Quickly Fix Common Windows 7 Set-up Problems

Even before you begin using Windows 7, you could be faced with installation problems that prevent you from correctly setting up Microsoft's new operating system on your computer. Once over the hurdle of getting it on to your hard drive, you may still have configuration issues, such as missing essential components.

If you've elected to upgrade your Vista computer to Windows 7, and have seen the installation process grind to a halt at 62%, then help is at hand! This is a common problem that sees the installation process freeze due to the failure of an essential service – the IP Helper Service to be exact.

Luckily, it is relatively easy to circumvent this bug by adding an environmental variable in Vista before starting the upgrade process – effectively ignoring the service when it crashes! Please note that this fix is for installations that stop at exactly 62%. To carry out this procedure, follow these steps:

1. After you have seen that your Windows 7 upgrade installation has frozen at 62% indefinitely, and will therefore not progress any further, eject your Windows 7 DVD and restart your computer.

2. Wait for your PC to roll back to Windows Vista. Click the **Start** orb, right-click on **Computer**, and then choose the **Properties** menu item.

3. Click on the **Advanced System Settings** option located in the left pane. Now click on the **Environmental Variables...** option.

4. In the System Variables section, click the **New** button to open up a new System Variable entry box.

5. In the Variable Name text box, type **MIG_UPGRADE_IGNORE_PLUGINS**.

6. In the Variable Value field, type **IphlpsvcMigPlugin.dll** and then click **OK > OK > OK** to close all the open screens.

7. Restart your computer via the Windows **Start** orb, making sure to re-insert your Windows 7 DVD. The upgrade process should now complete without freezing at 62%.

Restore Missing Windows Applications

Although Windows 7 comes with a whole host of new features, its installation has been streamlined by Microsoft. This tactic obviously saves on storage space, and optimises the Windows environment.

However, this increase in installation efficiency means that some of the programs you rely on, such as Windows Mail, Movie Maker, or Photo Gallery aren't installed by default. In order to install these missing applets, and more, follow this quick step-by-step tutorial:

1. To be able to download missing applications, you first need to go to the Windows Live Essentials website (http://download.live.com/).

2. Click the **Download Now** button to download a small installation program to your hard drive. Run this program to view the available applications.

3. By default, all the applications in the list will be downloaded and installed. However, doing this can get you a heap of software you don't need. Therefore, look down the list first and untick any items that you don't want. For example, if you don't use Windows Live to store documents online, then untick the **Microsoft Office Live Add-in** option.

4. Click the **Install** button and wait for the applications to be downloaded and installed.

5. On the next screen, untick the boxes next to **Set Your Search Provider**

and **Set Your Home Page**, if you don't want these settings changed. Click **Continue** to proceed.

6. If you decide at a later date that you don't want a particular application you downloaded, then you can uninstall it by clicking **Start > Control Panel > Uninstall a Program** and choosing it from the list.

> If you've just installed your Windows 7 system, you can find many of the missing tools from Vista from the Windows Live Essentials site.

Repair a Missing CD/DVD Drive in Windows 7

With Windows 7 finally installed, and all the applications you need set up, you may suddenly find that the CD/DVD drive you used to install Windows 7 has mysteriously vanished! Even if your computer's BIOS reports that all is good, this common annoyance with Windows 7 can stop you from using your CD/DVD drive for tasks like watching a movie, or installing other software.

Luckily, there is a quick registry hack that will have your CD/DVD drive back in no time. First, backup your registry by following the steps below:

1. Click **Start > Control Panel > System**.

2. Click on the link **System Protection**, then click **Create**.

3. Enter a name for your restore point, then click **OK**.

4. Once the restore point had been created, click **Close > OK**.

Next, apply the registry tweak as follows:

1. Hold down the [**Windows**] key and press [**R**] to open a run box. Type **REGEDIT** and hit [**Enter**].

2. Navigate to the follow registry subkey:
   HKEY_LOCAL_MACHINE\SYSTEM\CurrentControlSet\Control\Class\{4D36E965-E325-11CE-BFC1-08002BE10318}

3. Right-click on **UpperFilters** in the right pane and select **Delete**. Click **Yes** to confirm. If you see UpperFilters.bak, then just leave that entry.

4. Right-click on **LowerFilters** in the right pane and select **Delete**. Click **Yes** to confirm. If you see LowerFilters.bak, then do not delete this.

5. To complete the fix, exit the Registry Editor and restart Windows.

> Prior to doing any work in the registry, you should always make sure you create a registry backup, in order to recover your system if anything goes wrong.

Fix Problems When Your iPod/iPhone Won't Sync with iTunes

If you try to sync your iPod or iPhone with iTunes on Windows 7, you may see the following error:

```
iTunes could not connect to the iPhone because an
unknown error occurred (0xE8000065)
```

You can usually remedy this quickly by working through this troubleshooting table:

Possible Problem	Solution
Using an out-of-date iTunes version	Upgrade to latest version, restart Windows and try to synchronise again.
Firewall settings	Temporarily disable your firewall to check. Reconfigure your settings if this is the cause.
Verify the Apple Mobile Device USB driver is working – this can often be the reason why your Apple device won't sync	Go to **Device Manager**. Look in the **Universal Serial Bus Controllers** section. If this driver has an error symbol next to it, right-click it and choose **uninstall**. Now, click the **Action** menu tab and select **Scan for Hardware Changes**.

If the above doesn't work, then you may need to tweak the USB Power Management option via the Device Manager. To do this:

1. Hold down the [**Windows**] key and press [**R**]. Type **devmgmt.msc** and hit [**Enter**].

2. Expand the Universal Serial Bus Controllers section by clicking on the **+** icon.

3. Double-click on the first **USB Root Hub** entry in the list. Click on the **Power Management** tab.

4. Clear the box next to the **Allow the computer to turn off this device to save power** option. Click **OK**.

5. Follow steps 3 and 4 until all the USB Root Hub entries have been configured. Restart Windows and try to sync your iPod/iPhone again.

> If you are experiencing any USB device problems, adjusting the USB Power Management settings could help to cure them.

Revert to the Old Style Windows Interface to Use Programs Incompatible with Aero

The way Windows 7 looks is certainly impressive, but what if you don't like its interface and are much more comfortable using the old style, or you find that some of your older applications will no longer work with the Aero system? To quickly add a Classic Start menu and Explorer interface, use the program Classic Shell, which you can download here: http://tiny.cc/b4mpt.

This compact application adds these missing features, including a classic toolbar for Windows Explorer. To tweak your Start menu:

1. Click **Start > All Programs > Classic Shell** and select **Start Menu Settings**.

2. In the Controls section, click the drop-down menu icon next to the **Mouse Click Opens** setting and choose **Classic Menu**.

3. In the Skins section, click the drop-down menu and choose the **Classic Skin** option.

4. To display the programs that you regularly use in the Start menu, click the **Show Recent Programs** in the Show section.

Diagnose and Cure System Problems in Windows 7

5. In the Expand section, you can choose what Start menu items you want to automatically expand. For example, to be able to see the contents of the Control Panel in the Start menu, click the box next to the **Expand Control Panel** option.

6. Click **OK** to save the settings, and then try out your new Classic Start Menu!

To tweak Windows Explorer:

1. Click **Start > Programs > Classic Shell > Explorer Settings**.

2. To set the navigation pane style, click the drop-down menu at the top of the screen and choose **Windows XP Classic**.

3. To use large icons in Explorer's button bar, click the box next to **Use Big Buttons**.

4. To show free space and file sizes in the status bar, enable this option at the bottom of the screen. Click **OK** to save the settings.

5. Open an Explorer Window and then click **View > Toolbars > Classic Explorer Bar**.

Correct Problem-solving with the Windows Command Line Interface

Most of the time, the standard utilities that can be run via Windows' Graphical User Interface (GUI) will normally suffice for diagnosing and fixing general problems – for example, Check Disk.

However, when you need to drill down deeper in order to root out the cause, then you'll need to use one of the several utilities that are lurking under Windows' GUI. Keep in mind that some of the commands that you'll be using will require Administrator-level privileges. To elevate your level at any time in Windows 7:

1. Hold down the [**Windows**] key and press [**R**]. In the text box, type in **cmd** and press [**Enter**] to open a command prompt.

2. Type **runas /user:<useraccount>** "**<program>**" and hit [**Enter**] (e.g. runas /user:admin "chkdsk c:").

3. If prompted, enter you password or press [**Enter**].

> If you find that a command prompt command is refused because you have insufficient privileges, simply use the steps above to get the command to run as Administrator.

Crucial Steps to Troubleshoot Serious System Errors

There are a lot of meaningless errors that Windows can throw up leaving you wondering what to do next. In this section, we'll take a look at common low-level system errors that can be easily fixed with a simple command.

Fixing Windows Installer Error 1316

When trying to install, uninstall or upgrade software programs, you may see the following error:

```
A network error occurred while attempting to read
from the file C:\Windows\Installer\<file_name>.msi
```

If you're seeing this error, or a similar one to do with Windows Installer, it's usually the fault of a previously failed installation. To fix this problem, install the Windows Installer Cleanup Utility which you can download here: http://tiny.cc/7940y. Perform the following steps:

1. Click **Start > All Programs > Windows Install Clean Up**.

2. Select the name of the program you are having problems with ① and click the **Remove** button ②.

3. Click **OK** on the dialogue box and restart Windows.

4. When Windows is up and running, try to install, uninstall, or upgrade your software program as before – this process should now work.

Diagnose and Cure System Problems in Windows 7

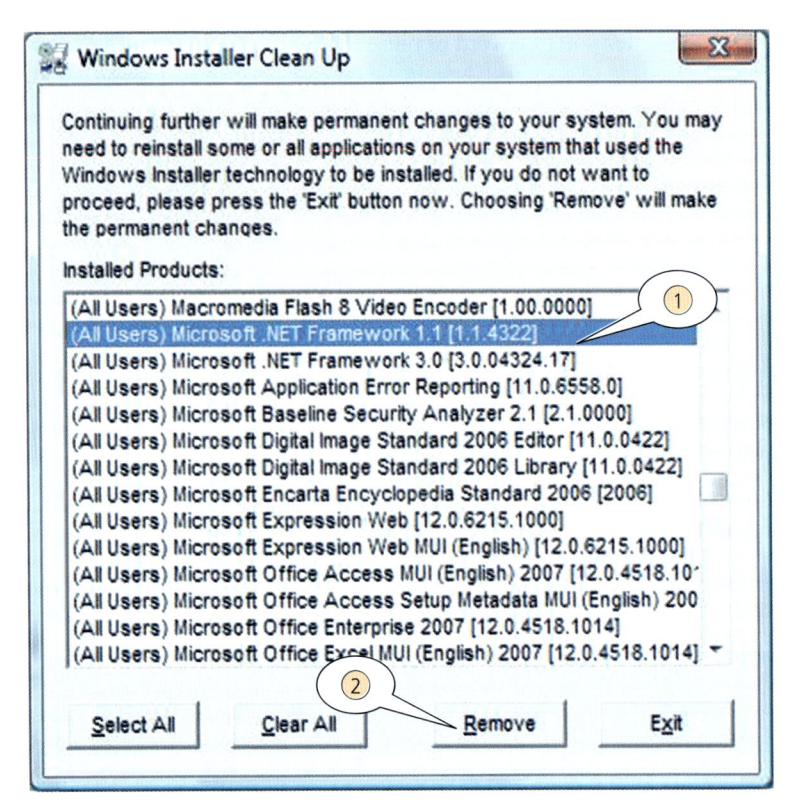

Clean your system with Windows Installer Clean Up

Resetting the Administrator Password

If you have forgotten your Administrator password and need to perform a task that requires elevated privileges, then unless you've got other administrative user accounts, you could be forced into repairing your Windows 7 installation.

One way around this is to use recovery and repair software. Trinity Rescue Kit is a program which provides you with an invaluable set of low-level tools, which you can download here: http://tiny.cc/2jniz.

This Mandriva Linux-based distribution has a great set of command line tools for working on your Windows installation. Before you can use it, you'll need to burn the ISO image to CD. To do so, download Active@ ISO Burner, which you can get here: http://tiny.cc/xrevq.

If you're going to use Active@ ISO Burner, install it and then copy the Trinity Rescue Kit ISO file on to your hard drive. Next, follow these steps to burn the image to a blank CD:

1. Open Active@ ISO Burner.

2. Click the **...** button to open a file browser and navigate to where you copied the ISO file. Highlight it and click **Open**.

3. Click the **Options...** button. In the After-Burn options section, enable the **Verify Data** function by clicking the box next to it. Click **OK** to save the settings.

4. Insert a blank CD, DVD, or Blu-ray disc, and choose the target drive to use.

5. Click the **Burn** button to write the ISO image.

> In order to reset the Administrator password, you will now need to restart your computer and boot from the CD – make sure the boot options in your BIOS are set to boot from your CD drive first. How you do this depends on the type of motherboard and BIOS that you have, so check with your PC's documentation.
>
> Generally, you need to press the BIOS menu key ([**F2**], [**F10**] or [**Del**]) then use the [**Up Arrow**] and [**Down Arrow**] keys and [**Enter**] to navigate to the Advanced BIOS Features menu. Set the first Boot Drive priority option to the CD-ROM drive, then press [**F10**] to save the changes.

To reset your Windows 7 password:

1. On Trinity Rescue Kit's main screen, choose the top menu item, or let it automatically boot.

2. At the command line type **winpass -u administrator** and hit [**Enter**] to reset the Administrator account.

Diagnose and Cure System Problems in Windows 7

3. Choose the number of your installation from the list (normally 1) and press [**Enter**].

4. To clear the Administrator password, press [**1**].

5. To re-boot your computer, hold down [**CTRL**]+[**ALT**]+[**DEL**].

There are many more uses for Trinity Rescue Kit such as recovering files and lost partitions, drive cloning (even over a network), self-updating anti-virus scanners, and more. To read the full documentation, type **trkhelp -l** at the command line.

Windows 7 can suffer a lot of problems that can't always be fixed using the general tools provided in the graphical user interface (GUI). By reading this chapter, you've been able to use a lot of powerful tools and techniques hidden inside Windows 7 to quickly diagnose and fix low-level problems.

3: Essential Steps to Remove Hard Drive Errors

If there's one part of your computer that can go wrong, it's your hard drive. Windows 7 relies on it to function correctly, and so taking the time to overhaul your hard drive will reduce the chances of losing your important data – not to mention having to install Windows 7 from scratch. In many ways, your hard drive can be compared to an engine of a car – it's a mechanical device that spins at thousands of revs per minute and contains many moving parts that will eventually wear out, resulting in mechanical failure.

If you've got digital photos, music, videos, movies, important documents, etc., then servicing your hard drive is essential to prevent data corruption or even loss. In this chapter, we'll show you how to monitor your hard drive's health and spot an impending failure before it happens; this will hopefully give you enough time to backup anything you haven't!

By following the step-by-step tutorials in this chapter, you'll also discover how to scan for serious errors, and delete duplicate files and junk that can waste an incredible amount of space. This chapter will also show you how to resize your partitions for effective space management in order to get the best out of your hard drive.

Prevent Data Loss: Diagnose and Fix Problems

The hard drive inside your computer is generally a very reliable component that usually lasts for many years under normal use. However, hard drives are also very complex and will eventually suffer some sort of failure. This part of the guide will show you ways to prevent data loss by diagnosing and fixing problems when they occur.

Spot an Impending Failure by Monitoring Your Hard Drive

Implementing a monitoring system to spot a hard drive failure is your first line of defence. Modern hard drives incorporate an early warning system called S.M.A.R.T. (Self-Monitoring, Analysis, and Reporting Technology) that you can use to predict if your hard drive is going to fail; this can give you enough time to backup your data before it's too late.

To use S.M.A.R.T., it has to be enabled in your motherboard's BIOS setting; consult your motherboard manual for more information. To start monitoring your hard drive, install CrystalDiskInfo which you can download here: http://tiny.cc/jirsy.

Once installed, follow these steps:

1. To make the program resident in memory, click the **Function** menu tab and select the **Resident** option. To make the program run at Windows 7 start up, select **Startup** from the Function menu.

2. On the main screen, the health status of every hard drive is displayed with a colour; blue indicates a healthy unit (1), while yellow and red show that there is a problem that needs further investigation. Click on the problem drive to see more information.

3. You can also set a temperature alarm if a hard drive goes above a set value. To set the maximum to 50 degrees celsius, for example, right-click on one of CrystalDiskInfo's system tray icons and choose **Collective Setting > Alarm Setting – Temperature > 50C**.

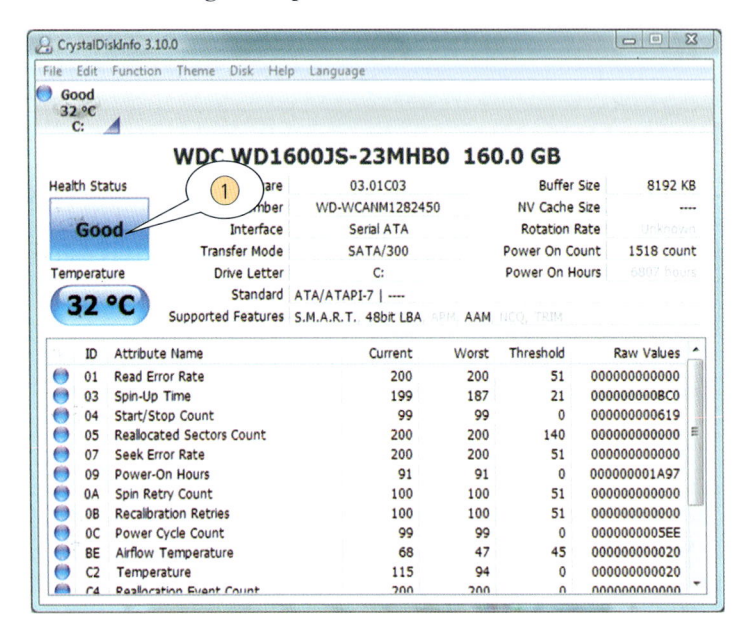

Monitor your hard drive's health with CrystalDiskInfo

Essential Steps to Remove Hard Drive Errors

> If CrystalDiskInfo reports that your hard drive is about to fail, then you will need to purchase a replacement drive and copy the data on to it from the old drive.

Deep-scan Your Hard Drive for Physical Errors

To properly overhaul your hard drive, you'll need to check for physical errors. Hard drives can develop bad sectors over time that need to be tagged so information never gets written to them. By marking bad sectors, you will ensure that your data is stored safely. To check:

1. Double-click on the **Computer** icon on your desktop to see the hard drive list.

2. Select a hard drive partition by right-clicking it and select **Properties** from the pop-up menu.

3. Click the **Tools** tab at the top of the screen.

4. Click the **Check Now** button, select both options and click the **Start** button to begin scanning.

5. If you see a pop-up message appear on the screen asking if you want to schedule a drive scan, then click on **Yes** to re-boot your PC.

6. If you don't get the previous message, then Windows will scan the surface of your hard drive for defects. Click the **OK** button on the message box, followed by **OK** on the Properties screen.

7. To check another partition, repeat steps 1 to 6.

> You need to regularly carry out this essential maintenance task (every 4–6 weeks) to avoid serious hard drive performance problems.

Free Wasted Hard Drive Space by Deleting Duplicates and Leftover Files

Space-hogging files can litter your hard drive and build up quite quickly, especially if you use your computer regularly. Fortunately, you can reduce the clutter by using free tools to quickly sweep out the junk.

Seeing Double? Delete Space-hogging Duplicates

You can increase your hard drive space significantly by removing multiple copies of files such as photos, videos, and music. You should download a program called Fast Duplicate File Finder, which will help you to free-up space on your hard drive. You can download it here: http://tiny.cc/6f8ml.

Follow these steps to search for replica files:

1. Click on the **Add Folder** icon and choose a folder to scan. To add more locations, repeat the process.

2. Click **Start Scan** ②. When this stage has completed, an information box will be displayed showing you how many duplicates have been found. Click **OK**.

3. Carefully go through the list of files to make sure that the selected items are ok to delete. Use the tick-boxes next to each file to select/deselect ③.

4. To delete the files to the Recycle Bin, click the **Delete Checked Files** button ④, followed by **Yes**.

5. If you want to move the files to a safe folder rather than deleting them straight away, you can click on the **...** button to choose a custom location. You can also make a new folder specifically for this task by clicking on the **Make New Folder** button. Once you have selected a custom folder, click on the **OK** button.

6. To move the files, click the **Move Checked Files** button, followed by **OK**.

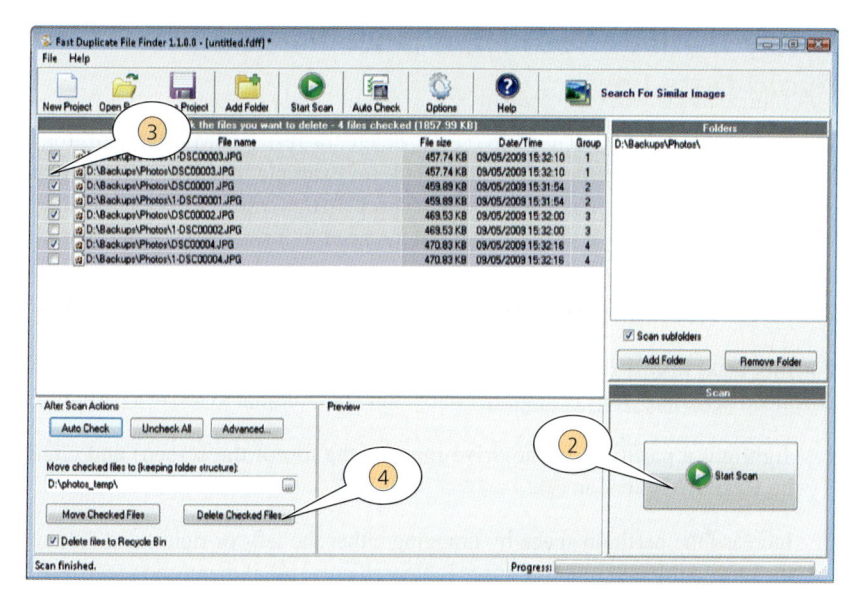

Remove duplicate files to increase hard drive space

> If you have an external hard drive, you can move the duplicate files to a folder on this drive, meaning that you don't lose them but that your hard drive space is increased.

Quickly Free-up Space Using Disk Cleanup

Window 7's built-in Disk Cleanup utility can help clean out redundant files that have been left on your hard drive. Disk Cleanup searches the Recycle Bin and other locations for unnecessary files. To use Disk Cleanup:

1. Click **Start** > **All Programs** > **Accessories** > **System Tools** > **Disk Cleanup**.

2. Select a hard drive using the drop-down menu and then click **OK** to start.

3. Select the items you want removed via the tick-boxes and click **OK** followed by **YES**. For advanced users there's also the **More Options** tab that you can use.

Essential Steps to Remove Hard Drive Errors   31

Safely Manage Your Hard Drive Partitions to Avoid Data Loss

There are times when you need to create, delete, or resize hard drive partitions for better space management. You may find, for example, that the partition that Windows 7 is installed on is running out of space. In this case, a partition manager will make resizing partitions easy without the need to format your hard drive.

How to Resize a Partition

For this task, install Easeus Partition Manager Home Edition which you can download here: http://tiny.cc/hrgmh. Follow this short tutorial to resize a partition:

1. Highlight a partition on the drive map (at the top of the screen) and click the **Resize/Move** icon ⑤.

2. Increase the partition space by dragging either the left- or right-hand-side of the map to use adjacent free space (coloured grey) ⑥. If there's no space, then you'll need to shrink an adjacent partition to free-up some space. Click **OK**.

3. To process the pending operations, click the **Apply** button. Some changes need to be made after a re-boot of your computer – do not switch off your PC while the partitions are being resized.

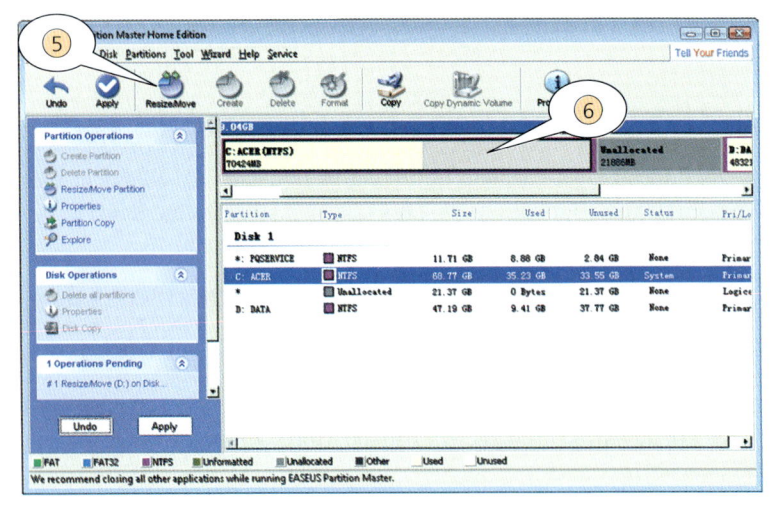

Use a partition manager to utilise hard drive space more effectively

Essential Steps to Remove Hard Drive Errors

> Creating different partitions on your hard drive – one to contain Windows 7 and one to contain your data – will mean that you don't lose any data if you need to re-install Windows 7 at any point in the future.

Fast Fixes for Hard Drive Maintenance Problems

Your computer's hard drive requires regular maintenance in order to keep it in good health. However, in certain cases, you'll find that the tools that you normally rely on won't be able to solve the problem. If you find that you have problems using the tools you need to repair your hard drive, follow the repair steps in this section.

Error: Disk Defragmenter Could Not Start

If you've tried to defragment your hard drive, but have been told by Windows that it couldn't start Disk Defragmenter, then the volume you're working on could be dirty! If a volume's dirty bit (that is the software switch that tells Windows to check your PC's hard drive for faults) is set, it could mean that its file system is inconsistent, or changes to the drive didn't get correctly written before the computer was shut down.

This is a fairly common problem that can be diagnosed by doing the following:

1. Hold down the [**Windows**] key and press [**R**]. In the text box, type in **cmd** and press [**Enter**].

2. On the command line, **type fsutil dirty query <drive letter:>** (<drive letter:> = c:, etc.).

3. If the volume is reported as dirty, then run **Check Disk**. This can be invoked at the command line by typing **chkdsk <drive letter:> /f /x** and hitting [**Enter**]. If Check Disk can't lock the volume, then it will ask if you want to schedule a check – type **Y** and hit [**Enter**].

4. After you have restarted Windows, repeat steps 1–2. The volume's dirty bit should now be reset – run Disk Defragmenter to verify this.

Free-up Space Occupied by System Restore Points

If you're struggling for free space on your hard drive and have used the Disk Cleanup utility, etc., you can shrink the space allocated for System Restore points to free-up even more of your hard drive. System Restore is much-improved for Windows 7 than in previous versions, but it can take up to 15% of your total drive space, or 30% of available space (whichever is smaller).

To resize this space allocation, follow these steps:

1. Hold down the [**Windows**] key and press [**R**]. In the text box, type in **cmd** and press [**Enter**].

2. At the command line, type **vssadmin list shadowstorage** and press [**Enter**]. This command will display your System Restore statistics.

3. It's advisable not to go too low for System Restore's allocated space because you still want a good level of protection.

4. To resize, type **vssadmin resize shadowstorage /for=c: /on=c: /maxsize=2gb** and press [**Enter**].

> Make sure you leave some space available so that System Restore can still work – at least 2 GB.

In this chapter, you've seen that monitoring your hard drive using S.M.A.R.T. can give you that much-needed time to backup your data before your hard drive fails. Checking for physical defects is also an essential task to carry out to prevent data corruption. De-cluttering your hard drive, especially removing duplicate files, can free-up a staggering amount of free space that you would otherwise have lost. And finally, using a partition manager to resize your hard drive's volumes will save you the pain of having to re-format your drive and starting all over again.

4: Dispose of and Cure Serious Network and Internet Problems

These days, using your computer often involves a good deal of time on the Internet. We have all become so reliant on using the Web for our daily needs that if something goes wrong, it can be a major headache – indeed, it's most people's number one reason for buying a Windows 7 PC. It's not always obvious what's wrong, and so this chapter shows you seven fast fixes for errors that can stop your computer from connecting to any type of network.

If you use Wi-Fi, then you'll probably already know that this type of network is particularly susceptible to interference that can stop you surfing when you least expect it. If you suffer from intermittent connection errors, then the Wi-Fi troubleshooting section in this chapter will be particularly useful. You'll also find a couple of essential registry hacks to get your old router working with your new Windows 7 operating system.

2 Quick Checks to See if a Website is Working

If you're having problems accessing a particular website and have ruled out your set-up, browser cache, etc., then you can use the Ping utility. Not only can this be used to test whether you can connect to another computer (a web server in this scenario), but it can also be useful in finding out a website's IP address and give you valuable information on network conditions.

To test a website in a command prompt window, type **ping <website address>** ① followed by [**Enter**]. For example, **ping www.windowsadvisor.co.uk** will tell you if the site's web server is up by displaying four replies ②.

> You can also use the displayed round trip times (in milliseconds) to see if there's a network problem between you and the website – the higher the number, the more latency there is which could indicate a problem somewhere down the line.

```
C:\Users\Mark-admin>ping www.windowsadvisor.co.uk

Pinging webcluster.gconnect.net [84.21.142.200] with 32 bytes of data:
Reply from 84.21.142.200: bytes=32 time=52ms TTL=119
Reply from 84.21.142.200: bytes=32 time=52ms TTL=119
Reply from 84.21.142.200: bytes=32 time=50ms TTL=119
Reply from 84.21.142.200: bytes=32 time=50ms TTL=119

Ping statistics for 84.21.142.200:
    Packets: Sent = 4, Received = 4, Lost = 0 (0% loss),
Approximate round trip times in milli-seconds:
    Minimum = 50ms, Maximum = 52ms, Average = 51ms
```

Ping a website to get advanced network statistics

Cure Difficulties in Accessing Certain Websites

While browsing the Internet, your computer builds up a local DNS cache to speed-up IP address resolution. The problem is, should this cache become outdated, or even corrupted, you might find that certain sites become inaccessible.

If you have several computers on your network and find that only one has this problem, then its DNS cache might need flushing. The best way to deal with this problem is to use the ipconfig tool. To do this, follow these steps:

1. Hold down the [**Windows**] key and press [**R**]. In the text box, type in **cmd** and press [**Enter**].

2. In the command prompt window, type in **ipconfig /flushdns** and press [**Enter**].

3. When this process is complete, the ipconfig tool will report that the DNS resolver cache has been successfully flushed.

> If these website cures don't help, the problem is probably with your Internet connection. Follow the steps in the next sections to resolve your network errors.

Discover the 7 Problems that Can Stop You Surfing

There are various reasons why your ability to connect to the Internet is hindered. It could be as simple as an unplugged or damaged cable (physical connectivity) to more complex issues such as a corrupt networking protocol on your computer. Here is a list of seven causes that can prevent you going online.

Problem	Description
Network adaptor issues	Usually a faulty device driver that stops hardware from working correctly.
Corrupt TCP/IP protocol	Prevents networking.
Winsock2 corruption	Core component essential for networking.
IP address renewal failure using DHCP	Without a renewed IP address, you will not be able to network.
Wi-Fi interference	Physical and electrical interference can cause signal problems.
Older routers can have compatibility problems with Windows 7	Some older routers don't support the new networking technologies built into Windows 7, resulting in network problems.
TCP auto-tuning in Windows 7	This TCP window size optimiser is incompatible with some older hardware.

The remainder of this chapter will focus on each of the above problems in detail and show you how to quickly fix them in order to get back online in no time at all.

Fast Fixes for Network Adapter Issues

In order for your computer to be able to network, you need to have a working device driver for your network adapter. Sometimes these drivers can become corrupted, which can result in non-functioning hardware (a network adapter in this case).

Before making any changes in Device Manager, it is advisable to first backup your network drivers. To help you do this, use Driver Magician Lite (DML) which you can download from: http://tiny.cc/xt20b.

Create a designated backup folder on your hard drive in which the drivers will be stored and follow the steps below to backup your network adapter drivers:

1. On the main screen you should see a list of drivers that are installed ③. For the purpose of this tutorial, only backup your network drivers; you can see which ones to select by looking in the 'Class' column for network drivers. Tag each one by left-clicking each box next to it.

2. Left-click the **Start Backup** button ④, choose the folder that you created to store the drivers, then click the **OK** button to backup.

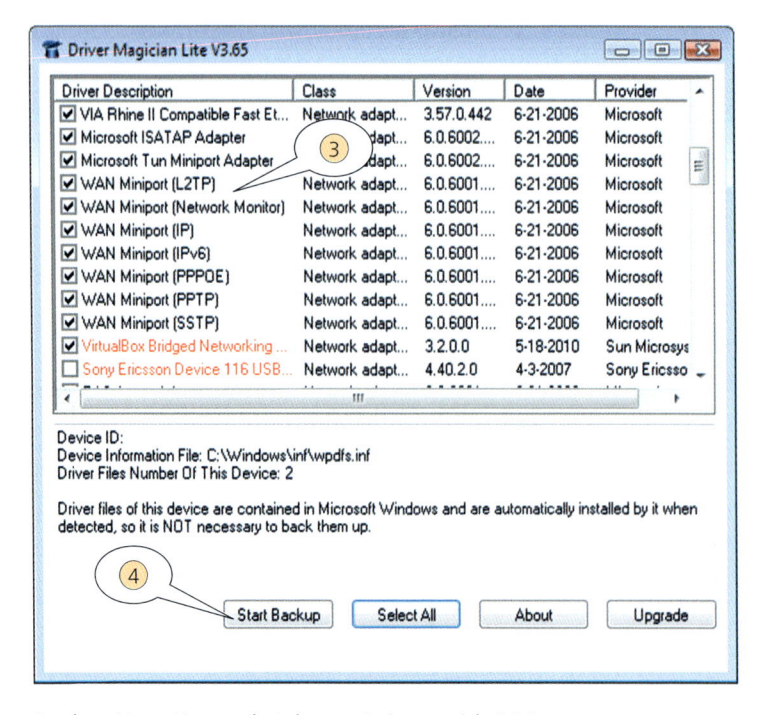

Backup Your Network Adapter Drivers with DML

For maximum security, consider backing up these files to removable media such as a hard drive or USB flash drive.

Now fix your driver issues using Device Manager:

1. On the desktop, right-click **Computer** and click **Manage** from the pop-up menu.

2. On the Computer Management screen that appears, click **Device Manager** (situated in the left pane).

3. If you see a device in the list that has a black exclamation mark in a yellow triangle then double-click on it.

4. Look at the device status in the pop-up window that appears. If the error is caused by a driver, click on the **driver** tab.

5. If you have downloaded a more up-to-date driver, click on the **Update Driver** button.

6. Errors sometimes occur when updating drivers to newer versions, if this is the cause, click on the **Rollback Driver** button to use a previously installed version.

> If you have missing or damaged driver files on your system then click the **Uninstall** button. Re-install the drivers to complete the fix.

Resolve Network Protocol Corruptions with Ease

Sometimes, the core Windows components that are necessary for networking can be corrupted. If this happens, you won't be able to access the Internet, a router, or anything on your network – this effectively isolates your computer.

There are two main areas of Windows that can suffer damage, which are the TCP/IP protocol and Winsock2. In this section, we'll show you how to recover these essential protocols without too much stress.

Checking the State of Your TCP/IP Protocol

To test your TCP/IP protocol and repair it if necessary, there are two low-level commands provided by Windows 7; these are: Ping and Netsh. Ping can be used to check that your TCP/IP protocol is functioning, and Netsh is a scripting tool that can be used to re-write two registry entries to fix the TCP/IP protocol. To use these two commands, follow the two short tutorials below:

1. Hold down the [**Windows**] key and press [**R**] to open a run box. Type in **cmd** and press [**Enter**].

2. In the command prompt window, type **ping localhost** and then press [**Enter**]. Alternatively, you can type **ping 127.0.0.1** to test the loopback address (if using IPv6, type **ping ::1**).

If your Ping is successful, you will see four replies. If you see a localhost unknown message, then you need to repair your TCP/IP protocol. To do this:

Dispose of and Cure Serious Network and Internet Problems

1. In your open command prompt window, type **netsh int ip reset c:\resetlog.txt** and press [**Enter**].

2. Restart Windows to complete the repair.

Winsock2 Corruption While Renewing Your IP Address

If you see the following errors (or similar ones) after using the IPCONFIG.EXE tool to release/renew your IP address, then you could be suffering a broken Winsock2 protocol:

```
An error occurred while renewing interface
'Internet': An operation was attempted on
something that is not a socket.
```

```
Internet Explorer: The page cannot be displayed.
```

Rather than having to complete a lengthy fix in the registry, you should download a repair tool called Winsock Repair, which you can get from: http://tiny.cc/19k57. Run the program and follow this short tutorial:

1. To see a list of installed LSP's (Layered Service Providers) and log them before fixing, click the **Show LSPs** button.

2. Click the **Repair Winsock** button to fix, followed by **OK** to re-boot (or **Cancel** to delay).

You'll also notice that the program can fix TCP/IP issues too – covered previously in our corrupt TCP/IP protocol tutorial. And finally, Winsock Repair also comes with a few useful tools in the Commands menu tab for DNS and TCP/IP tasks.

Cure IP Address Renewal Failure Using DHCP

If you suddenly find that you can't access the Internet or any other computer on your home network, then it could be that your IP address lease has failed to be renewed.

You can force the renewal process by using the IPCONFIG.EXE utility – this tool is also useful to see what's going on. By using this built-in command, you'll be able to see what IP address your computer has, whether it is connected to a DHCP server, and also force your IP address to be renewed if necessary. To do this:

1. Hold down the [**Windows**] key and press [**R**]. In the text box, type in **cmd** and press [**Enter**].

2. Type **ipconfig /all** to view the details of your Windows IP configuration.

3. Look for your IP address. If you find that your computer has an IP address starting with 169 or 0 (automatic private IP address (APIPA)), then you know that your machine isn't being allocated a network address by the DHCP server.

4. To fix this, type **ipconfig /release** and press [**Enter**], followed by **ipconfig /renew** and [**Enter**].

5. Wait a few moments and type **ipconfig /all** again. If this was the problem, your IP address should now change to the same subnet as the DHCP server (usually your broadband router).

To get a better view of what's going on, and be able to perform the above tutorial in a visual way, download AdapterWatch (available from: http://tiny.cc/pqqu4) to your hard drive and run. To release/renew your network adapter's address:

1. Make sure you are on the **Network Adapters** tab ⑤ and click the name of the adapter you want to work on at the top of the screen next to **Entry Name**.

2. Click **File** and select the **Release and Then Renew The IP Address** option.

Dispose of and Cure Serious Network and Internet Problems

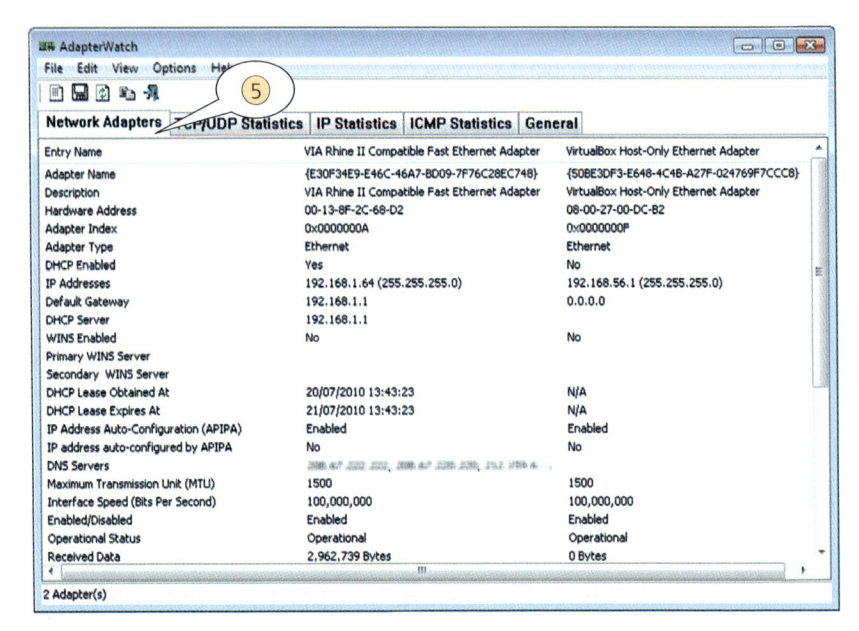

Use AdapterWatch to get the low down on your network

> You can use AdapterWatch to get a great deal of information about your PC's network adapters – essential when troubleshooting.

Trouble Going Online via Wi-Fi? Use this Fix

Do you have problems trying to access the Internet using Wi-Fi when the rest of the 'wired' computers in your home connect just fine? If you are having intermittent connection problems, high latency (lag), or at best slow throughput that makes it impossible to surf the Net, then this section will show you troubleshooting techniques to root out your wireless problems.

Optimise the Location of Your Wi-Fi Router

The biggest factor that influences the stability and performance of wireless networks is interference from various sources. Items in your home that could cause interference include wireless phones, microwave ovens, Bluetooth portable devices, and other electrical devices.

Even non-electrical objects in your home can affect the signal, such as metal cabinets, water pipes, and so on. If your Internet connection suffers from intermittent disconnections, or drop-outs as they are sometimes referred to, then you're probably receiving a poor signal. Work through the following table to help you optimise the position of your router:

Tip	Improvement on Network
Centrally locate router in your home	Signal strength evenly distributed – increased network reliability.
Keep away from other electrical items	Minimises electrical interference that can reduce network stability.
Avoid positioning near to surfaces that reflect	Maximises signal range and network speed.
Avoid physical barriers as much as possible; e.g. brick walls	Signal strength will be improved and network drop-outs reduced.

Sometimes simply moving your wireless router to another location in your house will result in a massive performance boost.

Monitor Your Wireless Connection Using InSSIDer

If you are suffering wireless connection problems and have ruled out local sources of interference, then it's worth using a third party utility to find out what's going on with your signal. If the problem isn't with your equipment, it could be interference from another wireless router – including your neighbour's!

To check on this, you can use the InSSIDer freeware program (which you can download from: http://tiny.cc/8i7s4) to check your signal. As well as having a realtime signal strength meter, the program is also useful for detecting other wireless networks that might be causing interference. To help you measure your signal strength, follow these steps:

1. Select your wireless network adapter from the drop-down menu at the top of the screen.

2. Click the **Start Scanning** button ⑥. This will start to measure all the detected wireless networks.

3. Keep InSSIDer running for a while to monitor your signal strength and its quality; if your wireless signal is weak, then you may see drop-outs on the graph (7). In this case, you may need to reposition your router, change router channel, or rule out interference from household electrical devices.

4. If you see other networks, then these could be interfering with your connection. Try logging into your router and changing to a different channel.

5. Click back to InSSIDer to see if your signal strength has improved. You may have to try different channels until you find one that gives the best improvement.

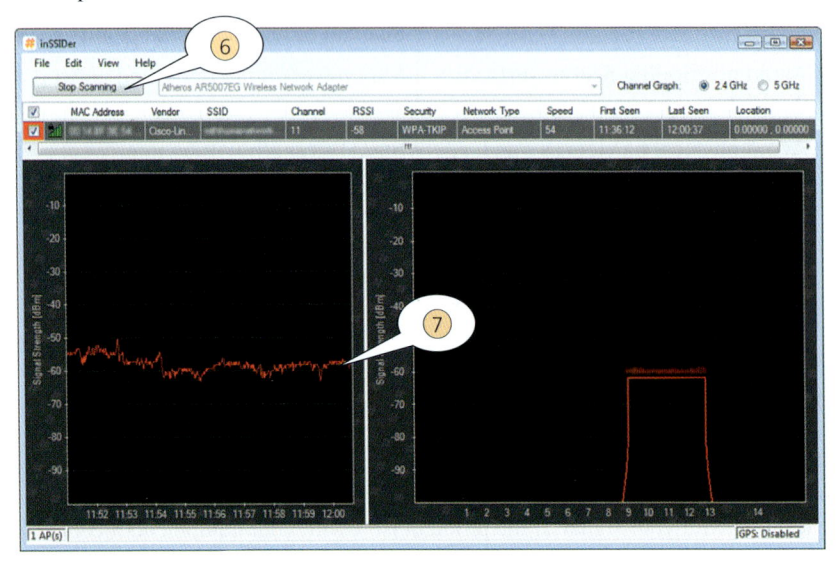

Use InSSIDer to check your received wireless signal

> InSSIDer is a great tool to help you find a nearby wireless network while you are on the move with a laptop.

Windows 7 Tip to Fix Problems with Old Routers

If you've upgraded your operating system to Windows 7 then your poor old router might not be compatible with the new networking technologies.

Fortunately, you can tweak your new operating system so you don't have to spend money on a new router.

The TCP Auto-tuning feature optimises your connection by automatically adjusting the TCP window size (RWIN). However, older hardware can be incompatible which can cause connection problems.

To disable TCP Auto-tuning:

1. Hold down the [**Windows**] key and press [**R**]. Type **cmd** followed by [**Enter**].

2. Type **netsh interface tcp show global** and hit [**Enter**] to display the TCP global parameters.

3. If the Receive Window Auto-tuning level parameter is not already disabled, then type **netsh interface tcp set global autotuning=disabled** and press [**Enter**].

4. If you need to re-enable TCP Auto-tuning in the future, simply complete step 1 and type **netsh interface tcp set global autotuning=normal**

There's nothing more frustrating than suddenly being unable to go online. By reading this chapter, you've learnt about the major problems that can cause your computer to lose touch with the outside world. You've discovered how to check and fix drivers, restore Windows' networking protocols, solve IP address renewal problems, work out your Wi-Fi connection issues, and apply registry hacks to make your old router work with Windows 7.

5: 7 Essential Tools for Windows Error Elimination

Windows 7 has its fair share of problems: error messages may be displayed, programs may crash and performance can be reduced, and it is often unclear what has caused the problem. Fortunately, there are a number of tools which can help track down the source of a problem which can make it much easier to prevent it from happening again. Read on to find out how to analyse and diagnose Windows errors – it is likely that there is no need to call in the experts.

Discover the Hidden Meaning of Cryptic Error Messages

When error messages are displayed by Windows 7, they are often incredibly cryptic and most people have a great deal of trouble interpreting what they mean – let alone working out what can be done to fix the associated problem.

If an error message makes clear reference to a particular program, it may be worth re-installing it, or at least performing a repair of the current installation of the software, in case any important system files have been overwritten or deleted:

1. Click the **Start** button followed by the **Control Panel** link.

2. Double-click the **Programs and Features** applet.

3. Select the program that the error message referred to and click the **Repair** button at the top of the dialogue box.

4. You may be prompted to insert the installation disc for the program in question.

5. Restart Windows. If the error message is still present, try visiting the website of the company who produces the software which is being problematic to see if there are any updates available or if a potential solution has been published.

> Not all programs have a Repair option, in which case they will have to be uninstalled and then re-installed.

Error messages relating to Windows itself are often the most difficult to interpret as they can contain error codes which are not properly explained. Microsoft has an online error message centre which can be used to help determine the root cause of an error message that has been displayed.

As well as problems with Windows, the Events and Errors Message Center (which can be found at www.microsoft.com/technet/support/ee/ee_advanced.aspx) also proves useful when diagnosing problems with other software produced by Microsoft:

1. Open a web browser and pay a visit to the Events and Errors Message Center.

2. Leave the first two drop-down menus so that the **--All Products--** and **--All Versions--** options are selected (1).

3. In the boxes labelled **Event ID** and **Message Text**, (2) type some of the information which has been displayed in the error message.

4. Click **Go** and a list of helpful online resources will be displayed that can be used to help fix the problem.

5. If you know that an error message is being generated by a particular Microsoft program, return to the front page of the Event and Error Message Center.

6. Use the first drop-down menu to select the program which is producing errors and use the second to indicate which version of the program you are using.

7. Enter any useful information from the error message and click **Go** to home in on helpful articles.

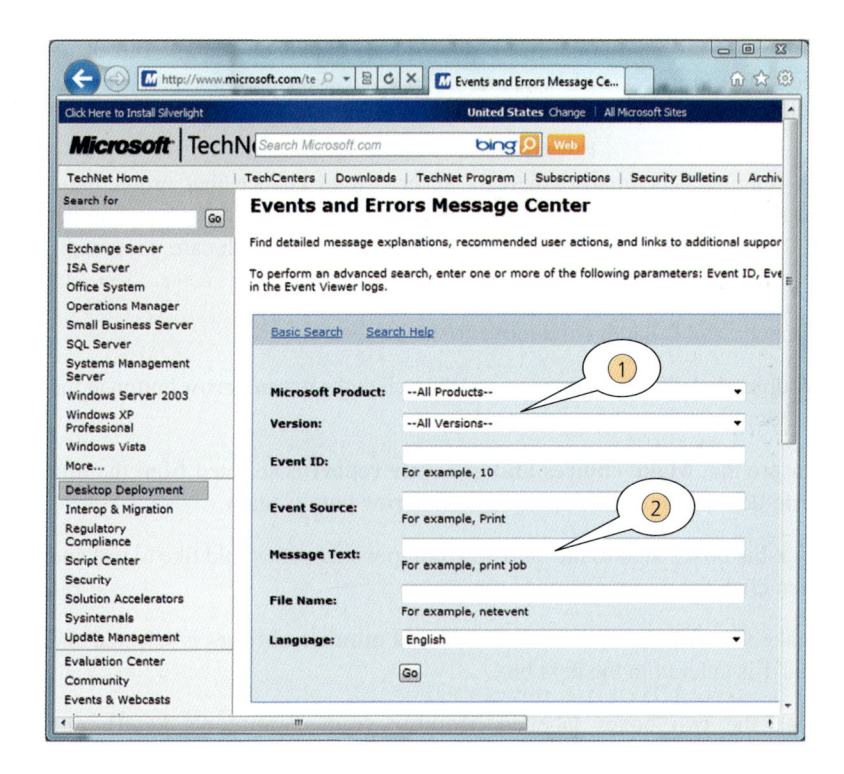

This online resource is regularly updated and is an excellent source of advice and potential solutions.

Cure Windows Problems Using SiSoft Sandra

When it comes to diagnosing problems with your computer, it makes sense to turn to a tool which has been designed with precisely that task in mind. One such program is SiSoft Sandra (with Sandra standing for **S**ystem **AN**alyser **D**iagnostic and **R**eporting **A**ssistant). A copy of the free Lite edition of the program can be downloaded from: http://tiny.cc/iujqe.

The program is made up of a number of modules and it is particularly useful for diagnosing problems with hardware – these can be notoriously difficult to track down until a particular piece of hardware fails.

7 Essential Tools for Windows Error Elimination   49

If a computer problem is hardware related, one means of tracking down the source is to run a series of benchmarks to test various components – this is something that SiSoft Sandra is able to do.

When running benchmarks, there is a very slight chance that problematic hardware may fail. Although the risk is fairly remote, do not run the benchmarks more than necessary to help avoid this possibility. Used with care, these tests can prove extremely useful:

1. Launch SiSioft Sandra and move to the **Tools** tab.

2. Double-click the **Burn-in** icon and then click the **green arrow** button at the bottom of the screen.

3. Ensure that **Make choices and generate report** is selected from the first drop-down menu and click the **green arrow** button again.

4. Tick the boxes next to the hardware components you would like to test and then click the **green arrow** button.

5. Make sure that the option labelled **Run a number of times** is selected and that **1** is entered in the next box.

6. Tick the two boxes labelled **Monitor your computer's health** and **Terminate on overheat/failure** before clicking the **green arrow** button.

7. Continue to click this button until it is no longer available and then click the **green tick** button to start the tests.

> Running the tests can be a lengthy process, but it is advisable to stay at your computer while they complete. Should an error message be displayed or a crash occur, make a note of which part of the test was running at the time as this will help to give an indication of where problems may lie – for example, if an error is generated whilst your hard drive is being tested, it is quite likely that there is a problem with the drive.

Solve Startup Problems to Fix a Non-booting PC

Programs that run automatically when Windows starts up can be the cause of numerous problems. As applications in the Startup section of the Start menu, as well as those controlled by certain sections of the registry, are not manually launched, it is not always easy to determine which one is to blame when one of them starts to be problematic.

While it is possible to manually work through the list of startup programs, things are made much easier by turning to Startup Control Panel. A copy of this handy free utility can be downloaded here: http://tiny.cc/629y1.

There are two versions of the program available, one of which does not require installation, but can be run as a standalone program. The second version, once installed, enables the program to be accessed through a newly created icon in the Control Panel:

1. Launch **Startup Control Panel** and notice the seven tabs at the top of the program window.

2. For now, the five tabs named **HKCU / Run**, **Run Once**, **Startup (user)**, **Startup (common)** and **HKLM / Run** are the ones we are interested in.

3. Click each of these tabs in turn and a series of programs which are configured to start automatically with Windows will be listed.

4. If you have been plagued by an error message which makes reference to a specific program, search through these five tabs for an entry relating to this program and clear the tick-box next to it by clicking it – this prevents the program from starting with Windows.

5. Close down the program and restart your computer. The problem will now be cured.

If a startup program that has been disabled is found not to be the cause of problems, it can be re-enabled by ticking the box next to it once again.

However, it is possible that any error messages that have been displayed at Windows Startup have not made explicit reference to a particular program. It is still possible to use Startup Control Panel to home in on which one is problematic, but the process is slightly lengthier:

1. Launch the program and move through each of the five tabs mentioned in the previous steps, unticking the boxes next to every item that is listed.

2. Restart Windows and you should find that an error message is no longer displayed.

3. Launch Startup Control Panel once again and move to the **HKCU / Run** tab.

4. Tick the box next to just one of the programs that is listed and then restart Windows again.

5. If no error message is displayed, re-enable another item which used to start with Windows, moving to one of the other four tabs if necessary.

6. Repeat this process, restarting Windows every time a program has been re-enabled, until the error message is displayed again.

7. It is safe to assume that the last program to have been re-enabled as a startup item is to blame for the error and it should therefore be disabled.

8. Right-click a program and select **Delete** to prevent it from ever running at startup again and then continue to re-enable the remaining programs.

> When disabling some startup entries, such as those relating to anti-virus programs, Windows may complain about missing security software – this message can be ignored for the time being.

This method of pinpointing a troublesome piece of software can be time consuming, but it is also very easy. It is worth noting that when a program is 'deleted' using Startup Control Panel, it is simply moved to the Deleted tab to prevent it from running.

If a startup program which has been deleted in this way is later found to be needed, move to the Deleted tab of the program, right-click the program in question and use the **Send To** menu to return the shortcut to the tab it originated from.

Repair Serious Registry Corruptions Before they Crash Your PC

Problems with the registry, the large central database of settings at the heart of Windows, can have wide reaching consequences. The registry is too large to manually check for problems, so it makes sense to turn to a dedicated error checking tool. One such program is Eusing Registry Cleaner and a copy of this free software can be downloaded from: http://tiny.cc/nzud0.

To use the tool:

1. Install the program and launch it from the Start menu.

2. Click **File > Backup Full Registry**, enter a name for the backup and click **Save**.

3. Click the **Scan registry issues** link ③ in the left-hand Tasks pane and wait while the program checks the registry.

4. Any problems that have been detected will be listed in the right-hand pane, with the first column, headed **Problem**, providing information about the nature of the issue ④.

5. When the scan is complete, tick the boxes next to the entries for the problems you would like to fix and then click the **Repair registry issues** ⑤ link.

6. Click **Close**, close the program and then restart Windows.

7. If there are any unwanted side-effects from fixing problems, the registry backup can be restored. Click **Action > Restore previous registry** and select the backup file that was created. You can then scan for problems again, but this time opt to fix only a few of them. This can be repeated as many times as necessary.

8. Should you find that a particular section of the registry is consistently flagged up as having an error, but you are not experiencing a problem, you can choose to ignore this item by right-clicking it once a scan is complete and selecting the **Add to Ignore Lists** option from the menu that is displayed.

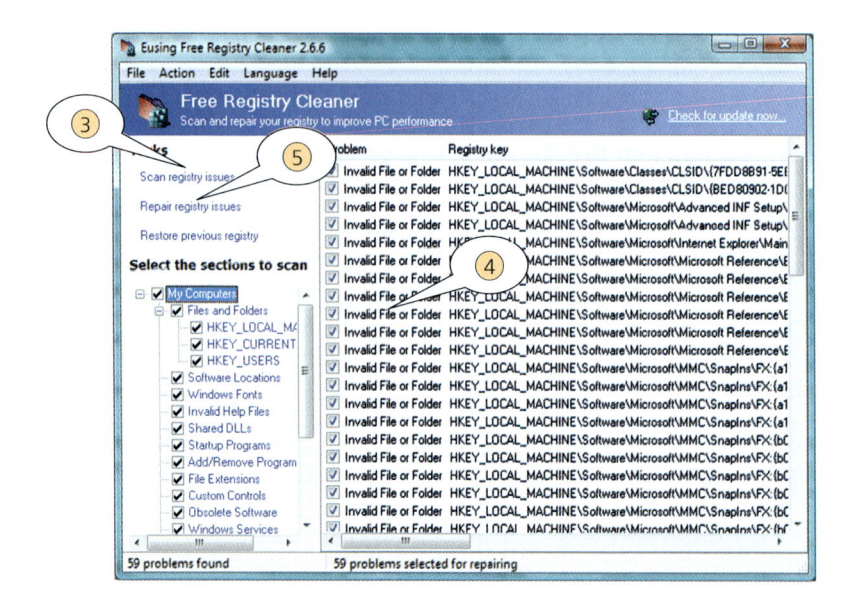

Fix Problems via the Action Center in Windows 7

Windows 7 includes a new tool which greatly simplifies the process of diagnosing and fixing problems that may crop up. The Action Center constantly monitors your computer and records any error messages that are displayed and logs any crashes that occur.

The idea behind the tool is very similar to Vista's Problems and Solutions Control Panel:

1. Click the **Start** orb and open the **Control Panel**.

2. Double-click the **Action Center** icon and any problems that Windows 7 has encountered will be listed in the window.

3. If a fix is available, the listing will be accompanied by a **View solution** link.

4. Click this link to view advice about how to avoid the problem in the future.

5. Older problems can be viewed by clicking the **Viewed archived messages** link to the left.

The Action Center can also be used to troubleshoot problems. This involves answering a series of questions to help Windows understand the nature of the problem, and possible solutions will then be suggested.

1. Right-click the **Action Center** icon in the notification area of the taskbar by the clock – if tray icons have been hidden you may first need to click the **arrow** button.

2. Select the **Troubleshoot a problem** option.

3. The troubleshooting tools are broken down into a number of categories – if the problem you are experiencing is listed, click the relevant link to be guided through the troubleshooting process.

4. Alternatively, click one of the five category headings to view additional problems and more troubleshooting tools will be displayed.

5. Many of the troubleshooters will cause Windows to run a series of diagnostic tests.

> The next time your Windows 7 system throws up a problem, try loading up Action Center to see if a solution is available.

Quickly Repair Corrupt User Profile Associations

This is a common Windows 7 problem which results in the loss of your user profile data and settings. When you restart Windows, you are suddenly faced with a new account! We can use the portable program ReProfiler, which you can download from: http://tiny.cc/05gv3. Create a System Restore point and then do the following:

1. In the top pane, click on the username that you are having problems with. To see its details, you can click the **Properties** button ⑥. Click **OK**.

2. If your user account has lost its settings and you see that it is now using a data folder ending in .000, then you'll need to assign it to your original data folder. To do this, click on the entry in the bottom pane that matches your username, but doesn't have .000; i.e. – a username called 'Fred' should be using a data folder called c:\Users\Fred.

7 Essential Tools for Windows Error Elimination   55

3. Click the **Assign** button ⑦, followed by **Yes** to confirm. Click **Yes** again to see the log file.

4. Click **Exit** and restart Windows.

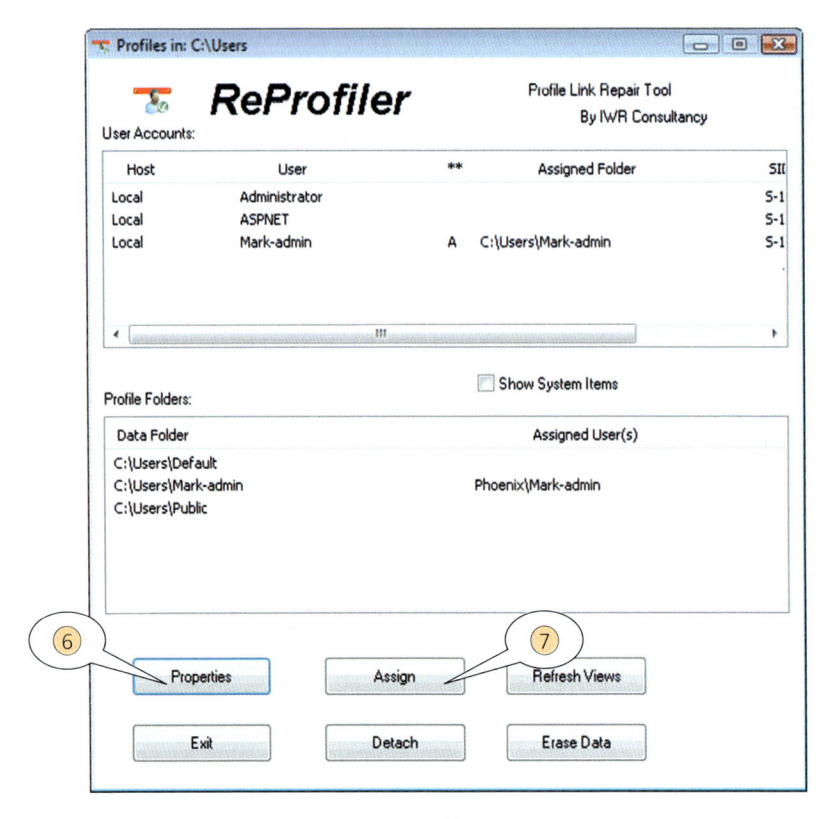

ReProfiler can fix broken user profile associations

Repair Audio Problems Experienced While Playing DVD Movies

If you're experiencing audio problems while playing a DVD movie (particularly on an older laptop), then it could be as simple as tweaking your speaker properties. The signs to look out for with this common audio ailment are either no sound, or audio that is inaudible.

The following tutorial will show you how to tweak your advanced speaker properties to solve audio issues with DVDs. To do this:

1. Click the Windows **Start** orb, followed by **Control Panel**. Choose the **Hardware and Sound** option and then click **Manage Audio Devices**.

2. Highlight the displayed Speakers device using your mouse and then click its **Properties** button.

3. Click the **Advanced** tab. In the Exclusive Mode section, untick the box next to the **Allow Applications to Take Exclusive Control of This Device** option.

4. Finally, click **Apply > OK > OK**.

If you've tried the above solution, but are still having audio problems with Windows 7, then it could be an audio driver issue. The Windows Automatic Update feature is an excellent aid to keep up with the latest security patches and fixes, but it doesn't cover everything.

In fact, unless you manually update some third party hardware drivers, they'll most likely just sit there hiding in the Device Manager. A good solution for updating these forgotten drivers is to use a software program such as Device Doctor (which can be downloaded here: http://tiny.cc/gdod7).

It will check all your drivers and update them to the latest versions – it can even identify unknown hardware. Make sure you have created a System Restore point as follows:

1. Click **Start > Control Panel > System**.

2. Click on the link **System Protection**, then click **Create**.

3. Enter a name for your restore point, then click **OK**.

4. Once the restore point had been created, click **Close > OK**.

Now you can run Device Doctor with these steps:

1. Run Device Doctor and click the **Begin Scan** (8) button to start scanning. When scanning has finished, Device Doctor will display a list of available updates that can be downloaded.

7 Essential Tools for Windows Error Elimination

2. Click on a **Download update** ⑨ button next to a driver.

3. Your Internet browser will open a new screen that provides a hyperlink to download the update. Click on **Download Driver Installer**.

4. Driver updates can come as an executable file that you can click on to install the new version. However, if the downloaded file is a .ZIP file then you'll need to open up this archive to run the set-up utility. For any other archive types, you will need to use an archive extraction utility.

5. Once you have downloaded all the drivers, install each one and follow the on-screen instructions. You may have to restart Windows several times until all the drivers have been updated.

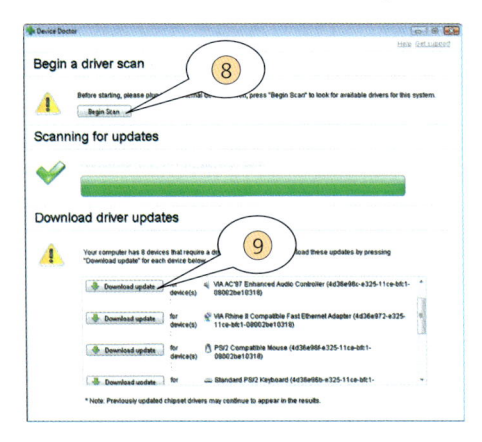

Keep your drivers up-to-date using Device Doctor

If you find that you download a driver package that Windows cannot uncompress, you should download and install IZArc from here: http://tiny.cc/5jieo.

There is no getting away from the fact that computer problems do occur, but the process of tracking down the cause may be easier than you think. Using a combination of tools built into Windows and third party software, you should be able to gain more information about the nature and causes of a problem which is a great help when it comes to diagnosis and solution.

7 Essential Tools for Windows Error Elimination

6: Safely Dispose of Windows 7 STOP Errors

Serious Windows 7 crashes – called STOP or Blue Screen errors – indicate that your PC is unstable, and that further more serious crashes are on the way that could leave your PC dead, with Windows 7 failing to start up at all. Fortunately, most Blue Screen errors can be cured quickly, and, if tackled at an early stage, will help you avoid more serious problems in the long run.

STOP errors indicate that something is seriously wrong with your PC and Windows can no longer continue running. If these errors occur frequently, it is a sure sign that your PC is heading for major trouble, and will soon only be good for the scrap heap. However, a STOP error will display lots of cryptic information that can help you get to the root cause of the problem – if you can decipher the meaning of the message!

In this chapter, we'll show you how to quickly interpret Blue Screen error messages from Windows 7 and get your PC back up and running in no time.

Dealing with the Dreaded Blue Screen of Death

An error that causes Windows 7 to crash with a Blue Screen error message, properly called a STOP error, but known to many Windows users as a Blue Screen of Death, indicates that Windows has experienced a serious problem. The causes of STOP errors range from badly coded software and drivers to faulty hardware devices, and the fact that your PC crashes without warning means that you can lose important data or your PC may be prevented from booting up.

Getting to the Root of Blue Screen Crashes

If your PC repeatedly experiences STOP errors, it is important to get to the bottom of the problem, before it gets out of hand and causes your PC to become completely corrupt.

When a STOP error occurs, it is important to make a note of all of the information listed in the error message, as it will help with troubleshooting. The most important line is the one that starts STOP, as this line contains the error code, which will help you find information about the cause of the problem. You should make a note of the numbers after the word STOP, and the four register codes following it ①.

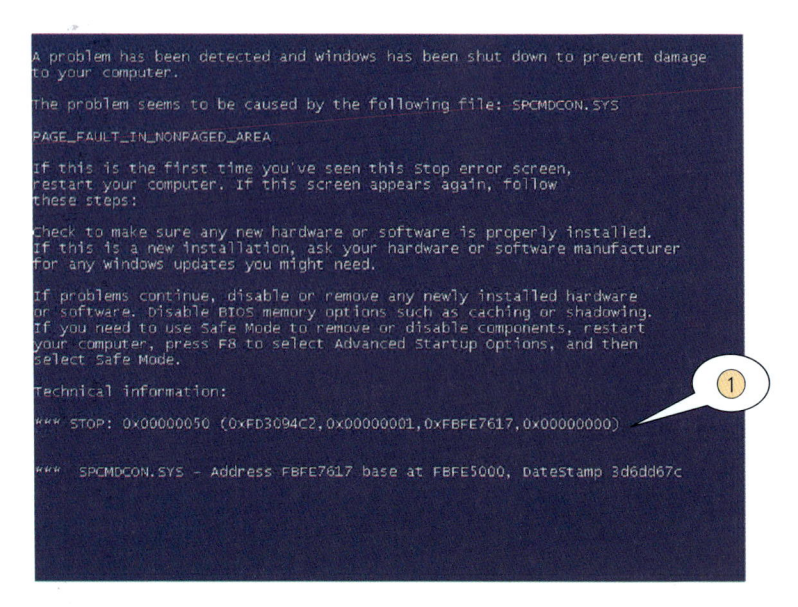

```
A problem has been detected and windows has been shut down to prevent damage
to your computer.

The problem seems to be caused by the following file: SPCMDCON.SYS

PAGE_FAULT_IN_NONPAGED_AREA

If this is the first time you've seen this Stop error screen,
restart your computer. If this screen appears again, follow
these steps:

Check to make sure any new hardware or software is properly installed.
If this is a new installation, ask your hardware or software manufacturer
for any windows updates you might need.

If problems continue, disable or remove any newly installed hardware
or software. Disable BIOS memory options such as caching or shadowing.
If you need to use Safe Mode to remove or disable components, restart
your computer, press F8 to select Advanced Startup Options, and then
select Safe Mode.

Technical information:

*** STOP: 0x00000050 (0xFD3094C2,0x00000001,0xFBFE7617,0x00000000)      ①

***   SPCMDCON.SYS - Address FBFE7617 base at FBFE5000, Datestamp 3d6dd67c
```

STOP errors list lots of details to help troubleshooting

Sometimes, the error message will contain the name of the driver or application that caused the fault. If this happens, then upgrading the faulty driver or program can often cure the problem.

> If a solution is suggested then your first course of action should be to follow it. STOP error messages can often be quite lengthy, so taking a digital photograph of your PC's screen is a good way to make a permanent record of the error.

Quick Cures for STOP Errors in Windows 7

If you are experiencing Blue Screen crashes, you can often solve the problem by running Windows Problem and Solutions Center. This Control Panel will check with Microsoft's servers to see if there is a fix for your problem, and if so, apply it. To use the tool:

1. Click **Start > Control Panel**.

2. Double-click **Action Center**.

3. Click **Check for solutions** next to the problem.

4. Windows will check for solutions to your problem, which may take a few minutes.

5. If you see the message 'No new solutions found', click **Close**. If any solutions are found, click on their links in turn and follow the wizard to apply the fix.

Essential Steps to Cure Serious STOP Errors

If the Problems and Solutions Center doesn't help, you will need to fix the cause of the STOP error manually. In this section, we have collected together fixes for some of the most common STOP errors you'll come across.

STOP: 0x0000C1F5

This error frequently occurs on Windows systems, and can be caused by corrupt Windows system files. When this crash occurs, you will see an error similar to the following:

```
STOP: 0x0000C1F5 (0x0000000, 0x00000000,
0x00000000, 0x00000000)
```

To cure this problem, you need to run the System File Checker as follows:

1. Click **Start** > **All Programs** > **Accessories**, right-click **Command Prompt** and choose **Run as administrator**.

2. If prompted, at the User Account Control screen, enter the administrator password or click **Continue**.

3. At the command prompt, type **SFC /SCANNOW** and press [**Enter**].

4. The System File Checker will scan your PC for corrupt system files and replace any that it discovers. You may be prompted to insert your Windows installation DVD during the process.

5. When System File Checker has scanned your PC, type **EXIT** followed by [**Enter**] to close the command prompt.

6. Re-boot your system for the changes to take effect.

> If you are having problems with a desktop PC, you can also try opening the case and ensuring that all cables, expansion cards and memory modules are properly seated in their slots and not loose.

STOP: 0x000000D1 DRIVER_IRQL_NOT_OR_EQUAL

This error occurs when your Windows 7 system attempts to access inaccessible memory. You will see a Blue Screen error message similar to the following:

```
STOP 0x000000D1 (0x0000000C, 0x00000002,
0x00000000, 0xF8E26A89)
gv3.sys — Address F8E26A89 base at F8E26000,
Datestamp 3dd991eb
```

If this error is caused by a faulty device driver, the driver name will be listed in the error message. If so, disable the driver as follows:

1. Press the [**Windows**] + [**R**] keys, type **devmgmt.msc** and then press [**Enter**].

2. Navigate to and select the problem device.

3. Right-click on the device name and choose **Disable**.

If this solves the problem, then you will need to contact the device manufacturer for an updated driver.

This error can also be caused by a very specific problem: if you have a system with a Pentium M processor, it may be using the wrong driver. To resolve this, first check which driver is in use:

1. Press the [**Windows**] + [**R**] keys, type **devmgmt.msc** and then press [**Enter**].

2. In **Device Manager**, expand **Processors**.

3. Right-click **Intel Pentium M processor**, and then click **Properties**.

4. Click the **Driver** > **Driver Details**.

If Windows reports that you are using the GV3.SYS processor driver, you must update to the INTELPPM.SYS processor driver. To do so, follow these steps:

1. Press the [**Windows**] + [**R**] keys, type **devmgmt.msc** and then press [**Enter**].

2. In **Device Manager**, expand **Processors**.

3. Right-click **Intel Pentium M processor**, and then click **Update Driver Software** or **Update Driver**.

4. If you are asked 'Can Windows connect to Windows Update to search for software?', click **No, not at this time** and then click **Next**.

5. Click **Search automatically for updated drivers** or **Install the software automatically (Recommended)**, and then click **Next**.

6. Click **Finish**.

STOP: 0x0000000A IRQL_NOT_LESS_OR_EQUAL

This STOP error indicates that a Windows component tried to access an area of memory that it was not authorised to access. When this happens you will receive a Blue Screen error message similar to the following:

```
STOP: 0x0000000A (parameter1, parameter2,
parameter3, parameter4)
IRQL_NOT_LESS_OR_EQUAL
```

If this error occurs, the problem could be due to an out-of-date Windows system. You should apply the latest fixes to your Windows system as follows:

1. Open Internet Explorer and click **Security > Windows Update**. Click **Check for updates**.

2. Click **Express**. The update wizard will check for the latest available updates.

3. Click **Install Updates**.

4. Once the updates are installed, re-boot your system, then repeat steps 1–4 until there are no more updates left to install.

> This problem can also be caused by a faulty hardware driver. If you have recently added a new hardware device to your PC, disconnect it and remove its driver. If the error doesn't reoccur, then the device is at fault. Contact the device manufacturer for a fix.

STOP: 0x00000050 PAGE_FAULT_IN_NONPAGED_AREA

This error indicates that Windows was searching for information in memory that was not found. If this occurs on your system, you will see a Blue Screen error similar to the following:

```
STOP: 0x00000050 (0xeb7ff002, 0x00000000,
0x8054af32, 0x00000001) PAGE_FAULT_IN_NONPAGED_
AREA nt!ExFreePoolWithTag+237
```

This error can indicate that there could be a problem with your system's RAM. This error can also be caused by a Trojan infection that implants a hidden rootkit to spy on your PC. If you receive the exact error message given above, this is likely to be the problem:

1. Open **Internet Explorer**. In the Address box, type **%windir%\system32\drivers**, and then press [**Enter**].

2. Look for a file named with a jumble of letters and ending with .SYS. The file will have a size of 14KB.

3. Right-click the file, and then select **Rename**. Rename the file **malware.old** and then press [**Enter**].

4. In the Address box, type **\WINDOWS\system32**, and then press [**Enter**].

5. Right-click on the file **MSUPD5.EXE** and choose **Rename**. Rename this file **msupd5.old**.

6. Right-click on the file **MSUPD4.EXE** and choose **Rename**. Rename this file **msupd4.old**.

7. Right-click on the file **MSUPD.EXE** and choose **Rename**. Rename this file **msupd.old**.

8. Right-click on the file **RELOADMEDUDE.EXE** and choose **Rename**. Rename this file **reloadmedude.old**.

9. Close Internet Explorer and restart the computer.

> After your PC re-boots, make sure your anti-virus software is fully up-to-date, then give your system a full scan.

Easily Cure Device-related Blue Screens

Many STOP errors are caused by problems with hardware devices. In this section, we'll look at how you can cure those hardware related problems to get your PC working again.

STOP: 0x000000ED UNMOUNTABLE_BOOT_VOLUME

This error message can indicate that you are using a standard 40-wire connector cable to connect your hard drive to your motherboard, or your BIOS settings are configured to force the faster UDMA modes. If this is the case, you will see an error similar to the following:

```
STOP: 0x000000ED (0xaaaaaaaa,0xbbbbbbbb,0xcccccccc,
0xdddddddd)UNMOUNTABLE_BOOT_VOLUME
```

To resolve this problem, you need to apply one of two fixes:

- Open your hard drive case and replace the ribbon cable currently connecting the hard drive to the motherboard with an 80-wire connector. These are available from all good PC hardware shops.

- Enter the BIOS menu for your PC by pressing [**F2**] or [**Del**] – the exact key to press will be displayed as your PC boots up. Use the [**Up Arrow**] and [**Down Arrow**] keys to locate the option to load the **Fail-Safe BIOS settings**, press [**Enter**] then [**F10**] to save the changes.

Safely Dispose of Windows 7 STOP Errors

STOP: 0x00000024 NTFS_FILE_SYSTEM

This error indicates that a problem occurred in the driver that allows Windows to communicate with your hard drive file system. This results in an error similar to the following:

```
STOP: 0x24 (0x000e0100, 0xf466a978, 0xf466a678, 0xf87c7625)
```

Usually, this error can be cured by using the Windows Disk Checker to repair your hard drive. To do so, proceed as follows:

1. Click **Start > All Programs > Accessories**, right-click **Command Prompt** and choose **Run as administrator**.

2. At the command prompt type **chkdsk c: /f** and press [**Enter**]. The Disk Checker will run, and may prompt you to re-boot your PC.

3. To close the command prompt type **EXIT** followed by [**Enter**].

> If the Disk Checker doesn't solve the problem, then you may need to backup and replace your hard drive. See Chapter 3 for details on troubleshooting hard drive errors.

STOP: 0x0000002E DATA_BUS_ERROR

The most common cause of this error is damaged system RAM modules, which means that data stored in memory becomes corrupt. This problem manifests itself with an error similar to the following:

```
STOP: 0x0000002E (parameter1, parameter2, parameter3, parameter4)
DATA_BUS_ERROR
```

If you have added a new hardware device to your system, remove the device and see if the problem persists. If not, then it is likely that the device was at fault. Contact its manufacturer to resolve the problem.

Crucial Steps to Cure Problems with the Windows 7 Kernel

The Kernel is the key component of Windows which is at the core of the operating system. Naturally, when Kernel problems occur, Windows 7 cannot carry on, and a STOP error results. Here's how to fix those problems.

STOP: 0x00000077 KERNEL_STACK_INPAGE_ERROR

This error happens when Windows tries to read data from the memory page file stored on your PC's hard drive but finds it can't. The error message will look something like this:

```
STOP: 0x00000077 (parameter1, parameter2,
parameter3, parameter4)
KERNEL_STACK_INPAGE_ERROR
```

To resolve this problem, first repair your hard drive with the Windows Disk Checker, using the steps given on page 74.

Next, recreate the page file as follows:

1. Press the [**Windows**] + [**R**] keys, type **sysdm.cpl** and click **OK**.

2. Click **Advanced**, then click **Settings** under **Performance**.

3. Click **Advanced > Change**.

4. If selected, untick **Automatically manage paging file size for all drives**. Select **No paging file** and click **OK > OK > OK**.

5. Re-boot your PC.

6. When your PC re-boots to Windows, press the [**Windows**] + [**R**] keys, type **sysdm.cpl** and click **OK**.

7. Click **Advanced**, then click **Settings** under **Performance**.

8. Click **Advanced > Change**.

9. Select **System managed size** and click **OK > OK > OK**.

STOP: 0x0000007F UNEXPECTED_KERNEL_MODE_TRAP

This problem is usually caused by a defective hardware device connected to your PC. The Blue Screen error will display information similar to the following:

```
STOP: 0x0000007F (0x000000XX, 0x00000000,
0x00000000, 0x00000000)
UNEXPECTED_KERNEL_MODE_TRAP
```

If you've recently installed new hardware on your system, the first troubleshooting step is to remove it and check if the error ceases to occur. If it does, the problem is likely due to the device, and you should contact the device's manufacturer to resolve the problem.

> You should also check your PC's cooling, as an overheating CPU can lie at the root of this error. Ensure that the CPU fans are turning, and that nothing is obstructing the flow of air through your PC's case.

STOP: 0x0000001E KMODE_EXCEPTION_NOT_HANDLED

This is one of the most common types of Windows STOP errors. It indicates that there was an error in the Kernel, which means that Windows can no longer run because the error hasn't been handled correctly by the program's code. This error will produce an error message similar to the following:

```
STOP: 0x0000001E (0xC0000005, 0xFCA733B9,
0x00000000, 0x00000000)
KMODE_EXCEPTION_NOT_HANDLED 0xC0000005 from
0xFCA733B9 (0x0, 0x0) Address FCA733B9 has base
at FCA70000 - SRV.SYS
```

Because this error can have many different causes, there are many different fixes that can be applied to resolve it:

- If the STOP error message reports that a hardware device is at fault, replace the driver of the faulty device with the latest driver version available from the hardware manufacturer.

- If no updated driver is available, try disabling the device named in the error message using the steps given on page 70.

- Check with the documentation supplied with any new hardware or software that you have installed to make sure that the product has been correctly installed.

- Check that the hardware devices attached to your PC are indeed compatible with your version of Windows, using the Hardware Compatibility List: (www.microsoft.com/whdc/hcl/default.mspx)

Fast Fixes for Driver-related STOP Errors

Faulty device drivers can cause all kinds of Blue Screen crashes. Follow the steps in this section to resolve those problems.

STOP: 0x0000003F NO_MORE_SYSTEM_PTES

This error occurs because an installed device driver is not freeing up sections of memory after itself – so called Page Table Entries or PTES. Even if the driver is not being used, it is holding memory open, meaning it is not available for other programs to use. If this happens you will see the following Blue Screen error:

```
STOP: 0x0000003F (0xA,0xB,0xC,0xD) NO_MORE_
SYSTEM_PTES
```

To resolve this error, you need to find the driver that is at fault, and either upgrade it or remove it. To locate the faulty driver, you need to apply a registry tweak. First, backup your registry as follows:

1. Click **Start > Control Panel > System**.

2. Click on the link **System Protection**, then click **Create**.

3. Enter a name for your restore point, then click **OK**.

4. Once the restore point had been created, click **Close > OK**.

Next, proceed as follows:

1. Press the [**Windows**] + [**R**] keys, type **REGEDIT** and click **OK**.

2. Navigate to the registry key: **HKEY_LOCAL_MACHINE\SYSTEM\CurrentControlSet\Control\Session Manager\Memory Management**.

3. Double-click on **TrackPtes** in the right-hand panel.

4. Change the Value data field to **1** and click **OK**.

5. Exit the Registry Editor and re-boot your system for the changes to take effect.

This will save the details of the driver that caused the crash in a special Windows debugging file. To interpret the file, you need to install the Windows Debugging Tools, which you can download here: http://tiny.cc/xjgft. With the tool installed, do the following when the STOP error next occurs:

1. Click **Start > All Programs > Accessories**, right-click **Command Prompt** and choose **Run as administrator**.

2. Type **CD "%PROGRAMFILES%\Debugging Tools for Windows (x86)"** and press [**Enter**].

3. Type **KD** followed by [**Enter**] to load the debugger.

4. At the debugger prompt, type **!sysptes 4** followed by [**Enter**].

5. Look through the debugger output for the name of the driver that caused the crash.

6. Close the Command Prompt window when you've identified the driver.

> Either upgrade or disable the problem driver to prevent the error in the future.

STOP: 0x000000EA THREAD_STUCK_IN_DEVICE_DRIVER

This problem is caused by a Windows device driver causing the system to pause indefinitely. Usually, the driver at fault is the graphics card driver, and will cause an error, similar to the following:

```
STOP: 0x000000EA, (0x81774538,0x81a8fc78,0x8193e4
90, 0x00000001) THREAD_STUCK_IN_DEVICE_DRIVER
```

To solve this problem, upgrade your video driver to the latest version available from your graphics card manufacturer. If the problem persists, do the following:

1. Click **Start > Control Panel > Display**.

2. Click the **Settings** tab, click **Advanced**.

3. Click the **Troubleshoot** tab.

4. Move the **Hardware Acceleration** slider to **None**, and untick **Enable write combining**.

5. Click **OK > OK**.

Prevent Constant Windows 7 Re-boots Caused by Blue Screen Crashes

If you find your PC constantly re-boots, it could be that a STOP error is occurring, but your PC is configured to re-boot automatically instead of displaying the error. In order to display the error to discover its root cause, follow these steps:

1. Press the **[Windows]** + **[R]** keys, type **sysdm.cpl** and click **OK**.

2. Click the **Advanced** tab then click **Settings** under **Startup and Recovery**.

3. Untick **Automatically restart**.

4. Click **OK > OK**.

> STOP errors can cause serious PC problems, from the loss of important data, to a PC that will no longer boot. This is why it is important to get to the bottom of a STOP error as soon as it occurs, and fix the problem before it gets out of hand. In this chapter, we've shown you some of the major STOP errors you're likely to come across in Windows and, most importantly, how to fix them with a minimum of fuss.

Safely Dispose of Windows 7 STOP Errors

7: Quickly Repair Problems with DLL Files in Windows 7

In order to save time when writing applications, software developers use code 'libraries' that store common functions and routines, meaning that each developer doesn't have to re-invent the wheel each time they write a program. This has many benefits, such as a common look and feel for Windows, since each application uses the same library code to draw a window or display a menu.

However, problems with these shared pieces of code, called Dynamic Link Libraries or DLLs in Windows, can lead to all kinds of mysterious errors. A DLL problem will affect every application that depends on that DLL, meaning that errors soon get out of hand.

While certain system protection features mean that Windows 7 doesn't suffer from the same scale of problems that Windows 98 and Me did, DLL problems can still cause havoc. Fortunately, we'll show you how to deal with the most serious DLL errors in this chapter.

Getting to the Bottom of DLL Errors

DLL files are essential components of Windows, and virtually every PC application that you will ever use. Because they are so fundamental to your PC's operation, they can also be the source of many serious system errors, and depending on which DLL file is at fault, it can leave all of the applications on your PC that depend on it not working.

DLL problems come in a range of shapes and sizes. Missing DLL files are usually the easiest to fix, since the name of the missing file is usually given in the problem's error message, allowing you to track down and replace the file. Problems caused by incorrect versions of the DLL files are more difficult to resolve, since the required DLL file will be present on your system, but the version number will be wrong.

> More often than not, these problems can be quickly resolved by re-installing the affected application, to force the required DLLs to be re-installed.

Avoid DLL Problems Before they Get Nasty

They say that prevention is the best medicine, and this is definitely the case where DLL files are concerned. Try to follow the steps below to avoid DLL problems before they happen:

- When installing an application, be careful if it asks you whether to remove a shared DLL file. If in doubt, always answer 'No'.

- Keep Windows and your applications up-to-date with the latest bug fixes and patches. The latest Windows patches can be installed via **Start > All Programs > Windows Update**.

- Ensure your anti-virus and anti-spyware tools are up-to-date and running to prevent malicious software from damaging the DLL files on your system.

3 Quick Fixes to Resolve DLL Errors

If your PC is playing up and displaying error messages that relate to DLL files, there are a few quick fixes you can apply that will resolve the vast majority of problems.

Fix 1: Re-install Faulty Software

Uninstall the application that is causing the problem using the Control Panel, then re-install it from its original CD or SETUP.EXE file. Not only will this replace any corrupt DLL files, but it will also correct any corrupt registry entries.

Fix 2: Use System Restore

If the DLL problem you are experiencing started when you installed a new piece of software or hardware, System Restore will help get your PC back to its previous working configuration. You can switch your PC back to its earlier set-up as follows:

1. Click **Start > All Programs > Accessories > System Tools > System Restore**. Click **Next**.

2. Select **Choose a different restore point** and click **Next**.

3. Choose the restore point you would like to use by clicking on it. Click **Next**.

4. Click **Finish**. The system will be restored to its previous state.

Fix 3: Find a New Copy of the DLL

If you've tried the two steps above to no avail, you should next try downloading a fresh copy of the DLL file from the Internet and saving it to your PC in the correct location. Browse to the site: www.dll-downloads.com/. From here, you can search for and download hundreds of DLL files. Check the README.TXT file in the DLL Zip archive that you download to check where the DLL needs to be placed on your hard drive.

> Installing the DLL file is as simple as copying into the folder listed in the README.TXT file.

Stop Orphaned DLLs Cluttering Your System with DLLArchive

One of the problems with DLL files is that application developers very often leave them lying around on a system when they are not needed. When you uninstall an application, often it will leave behind some of its DLL files. Over time, these orphaned DLLs will build up, cluttering up your drive and wasting hard drive space, and also potentially conflicting with other applications.

DLLArchive (which you can download from: http://tiny.cc/ozfm7) can help cure the problem. It works by scanning your PC for DLL files, and then checks the programs on your PC to see if any of them are using the DLLs found. Any DLLs that are discovered that are not being used are displayed in the main program window.

From here you can move them to a temporary archive. Here's how:

1. Click **Start > All Programs > AnalogX**, right-click on **DLLArchive** and choose **Run as administrator**.

2. Click **Search** ①.

3. Once the search is complete, you will be presented with a list of the orphaned DLLs. Click **Archive All** ② to archive them.

Quickly Repair Problems with DLL Files in Windows 7

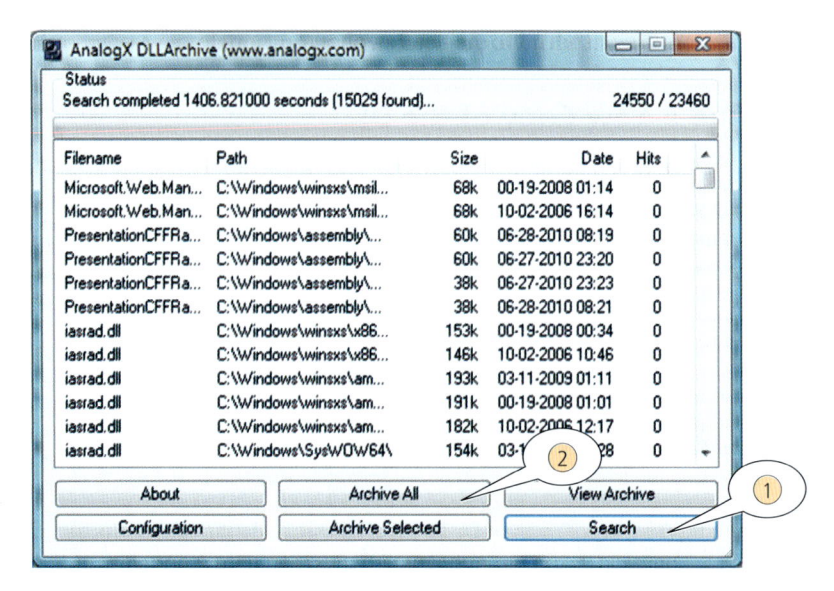

Archive redundant DLL files

> If you find that a program actually needs a DLL that has been moved to the archive, because the program generates an error message, simply click **View Archive**, select the required file and click **Restore Selected**.

If you find that no DLL-related error messages pop-up a month after you've archived the orphaned DLLs, it is usually safe to remove them from your system. The DLL files can be found in a subdirectory of the Windows folder, from where they can be safely backed up to CD/DVD and then deleted from your system. To do so:

1. Open **Computer** and navigate to **C:\Windows\DLLArchive** (3).

2. Press [**Ctrl**] + [**A**] to select all the files, then check the total size of the files selected at the bottom of the window. If the size of the files is greater than 640 MB, you will need to burn the data to DVD, otherwise a CD will do.

3. Insert an appropriate blank disc into your CD/DVD burner and click **Burn** (4).

4. Enter a name for the disc (e.g. **DLL Backup**) and, if available, ensure that the type is set to **Mastered** rather than Live File System. You may need to expand the **Show formatting options** heading to see this.

Quickly Repair Problems with DLL Files in Windows 7

5. Click **Next** and the disc will be burned.

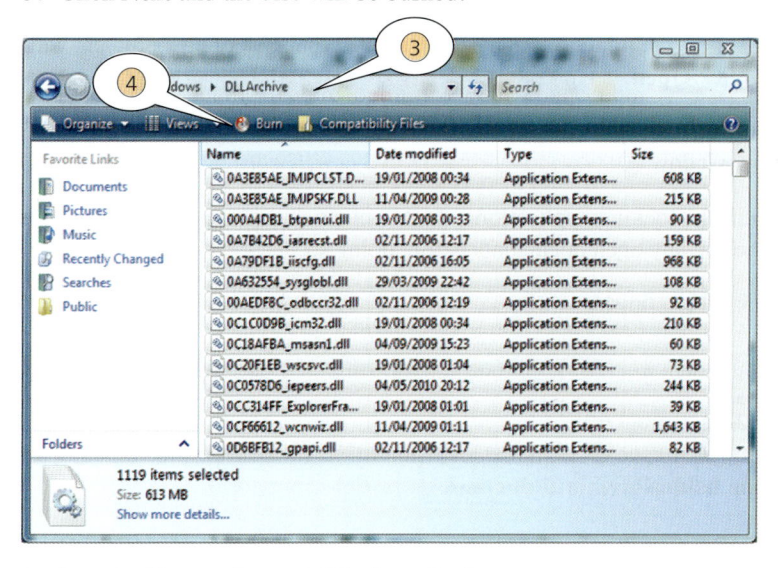

Backup the files to disc with Windows Explorer

Once the DLL files are backed up on to CD/DVD, you can delete them by moving them to the Recycle Bin as you would any other file.

Cure Problems with Locked DLL Files

If you find that you're having problems with a DLL file – for example, it is reported as being the wrong version – then replacing the file with a new version can often help. However, you may find that when you try to copy, move or delete a DLL file, you see an error message telling you that the file is in use and cannot be moved.

If this happens, then you need to use a free tool called Who's Locking, which you can download from: http://tiny.cc/a9fds. It will tell you which applications are currently locking the file you are having problems with, and allow you to quickly kill those applications. To use the tool, follow these steps:

Quickly Repair Problems with DLL Files in Windows 7

1. Open **Who's Locking**.

2. Click the **...** button, browse for the DLL file you are having a problem with and click **Open**.

3. Click **Refresh** ⑤. Any applications locking the file will be shown in the main window ⑥.

4. To kill the locking applications, double-click on each in turn – make sure you close any open documents before doing so.

5. Click **OK** to finish.

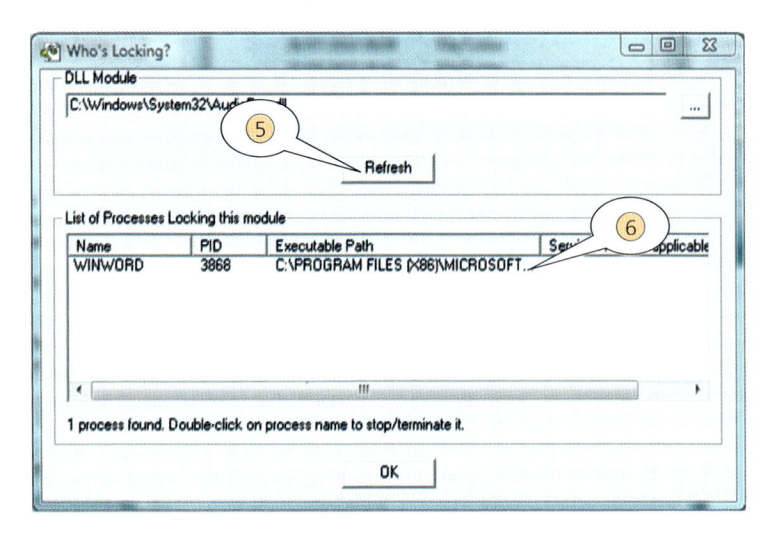

Unlock problem DLL files with Who's Locking

With the problem file unlocked, you can now replace, copy or move it.

Re-register Missing DLLs with RegSvr32

Even if all required DLL files are present and correct on your system, you can still experience DLL-related errors. In many cases, DLL files need to be registered with Windows before they are accessible, and if they are not registered errors will be thrown up.

Unfortunately, these errors are usually quite cryptic, and often don't give details of which DLL file is at fault. We've collected together some of the most common DLL-related problems below.

Fix ActiveX-related DLL Errors

When you try to run an ActiveX Data Object (ADO), which often feature as part of interactive websites, you may find an error message is displayed when the ADO tries to connect to a database. The error message looks something like this:

```
ADODB.Connection error '800a0e7a'
ADO could not find the specified provider.
```

This error occurs because the MSDASQL.DLL file is either unavailable or is not registered. This can be caused by an incomplete upgrade or a bad installation of the Microsoft Data Access Components (MDAC).

To cure the problem, follow these steps:

1. Press the [**Windows**] +[**R**] keys.

2. In the Run box, type **REGSVR32 "C:\Program Files\Common Files\System\ole db\MSDASQL.DLL"**.

3. Click **OK**.

Cure Runtime Error R6025 -Pure Virtual Function Call

If you use Microsoft Money and try to update your system with online quotes, you may see the following Microsoft Visual C++ Runtime Library error message:

```
Runtime Error!
Program: C:\Program Files\Microsoft Money\
MSMONEY.EXE
R6025 -pure virtual function call
```

To cure this problem, you need to re-register a series of DLL files that the system can no longer access. To do so, follow these steps:

1. Click **Start > All Programs > Accessories**. Right-click on **Command Prompt** and choose **Run as administrator**.

2. At the command prompt type **regsvr32 rsabase.dll**, and then press [**Enter**]. Click **OK**.

3. Type **regsvr32 softpub.dll** and press [**Enter**]. Click **OK**.

4. Type **regsvr32 wintrust.dll** and press [**Enter**]. Click **OK**.

5. Type **regsvr32 initpki.dll** and press [**Enter**]. Click **OK**.

6. Type **regsvr32 dssenh.dll** and press [**Enter**]. Click **OK**.

7. Type **regsvr32 rsaenh.dll** and press [**Enter**]. Click **OK**.

8. Type **regsvr32 cryptdlg.dll** and press [**Enter**]. Click **OK**.

9. Type **regsvr32 gpkcsp.dll** and press [**Enter**]. Click **OK**.

10. Type **regsvr32 sccbase.dll** and press [**Enter**]. Click **OK**.

11. Type **regsvr32 slbcsp.dll** and press [**Enter**]. Click **OK**.

12. Type **EXIT** and press [**Enter**].

Fix Problems with Secure Websites in Internet Explorer

If you find that Internet Explorer will not allow you to log-on to secure websites, it could mean that you can't safely access essential services such as online banking. If so, the problem is probably due to unregistered DLL files.

To fix this problem you need to re-register the Internet Explorer DLL files. To do this, follow these steps:

1. Click **Start > All Programs > Accessories**. Right-click on **Command Prompt** and choose **Run as administrator**.

2. At the command prompt type: **regsvr32 softpub.dll** and press [**Enter**]. Click **OK**.

3. Type **regsvr32 wintrust.dll** and press [**Enter**]. Click **OK**.

4. Type **regsvr32 initpki.dll** and press [**Enter**]. Click **OK**.

5. Type **regsvr32 dssenh.dll** and press [**Enter**]. Click **OK**.

6. Type **regsvr32 rsaenh.dll** and press [**Enter**]. Click **OK**.

7. Type **regsvr32 gpkcsp.dll** and press [**Enter**]. Click **OK**.

8. Type **regsvr32 sccbase.dll** and press [**Enter**]. Click **OK**.

9. Type **regsvr32 slbcsp.dll** and press [**Enter**]. Click **OK**.

10. Type **regsvr32 cryptdlg.dll** and press [**Enter**]. Click **OK**.

11. Type **regsvr32 mssip32.dll** and press [**Enter**]. Click **OK**.

12. Type **EXIT** and click **OK**.

> If you find that Internet Explorer is causing lots of error messages, re-registering the DLL files by following the steps above can often help.

DLLs are essential components of Windows 7, but they can be at the root of many mysterious system and application errors. If you're having problems with your system, look out for error messages that state a DLL file is at fault. Armed with the troubleshooting steps in this chapter, you'll have the problem fixed in no time.